The Miracle of
CHRISTMAS

STORMIE
OMARTIAN

HARVEST HOUSE PUBLISHERS

Scripture quotations are taken from the New King James Version. Copyright ©1982 by Thomas Nelson, Inc. Used by permission. All rights reserved.

Cover by Koechel Peterson & Associates, Inc., Minneapolis, Minnesota

Back cover author photo © Michael Gomez Photography

THE MIRACLE OF CHRISTMAS
Previously published as *The Power of Christmas Prayer*™
Copyright © 2000 by Stormie Omartian
Published by Harvest House Publishers
Eugene, Oregon 97402
www.harvesthousepublishers.com

ISBN 978-0-7369-5174-6 (pbk.)
ISBN 978-0-7369-5176-0 (eBook)

The Library of Congress has cataloged this edition as follows:

Omartian, Stormie.
The power of Christmas prayer / Stormie Omartian.
   p. cm.
Includes bibliographical references.
ISBN 0-7369-1004-2
   1. Christmas—Prayer-books and devotions—English. I. Title.
BV45.O63 2003
242'.335—dc21

2003001998

Printed in the United States of America

12 13 14 15 16 17 18 19 20 / BP-MS / 10 9 8 7 6 5 4 3 2 1

Acknowledgments

With special thanks:
To Michael Omartian,
Susan Martinez,
Katie Stewart, and Roz Thompson,
for praying this book into being.

To Bob Hawkins Jr.,
Carolyn McCready,
Barb Sherrill, and the people
at Harvest House,
for making it happen.

To the Reader

This account of the birth of Christ is based on several Bible translations of the first and second chapters of Matthew and Luke, and the prophecies of Isaiah, Micah, and Jeremiah. I have also included specifics about the culture, geography, people, and government of that time according to a number of excellent historians and writers of Bible commentary. In cases where the experts did not agree, I made choices as to the details I included. These details do not affect the profound impact of the story one way or the other, except to provide a clearer picture of what life was like at the time. I have also taken the liberty of exploring the possible reactions, perceptions, and actions of the characters involved and coming to a conclusion about what they may have been thinking, feeling, doing, or saying in response to what was happening to them. While Scripture guides us in the basic story line, the inner workings of these individuals and the daily details of their lives are left to the imagination. But inherent in the characters and events of this first Christmas is a message for each one of us that is something worth praying about.

Contents

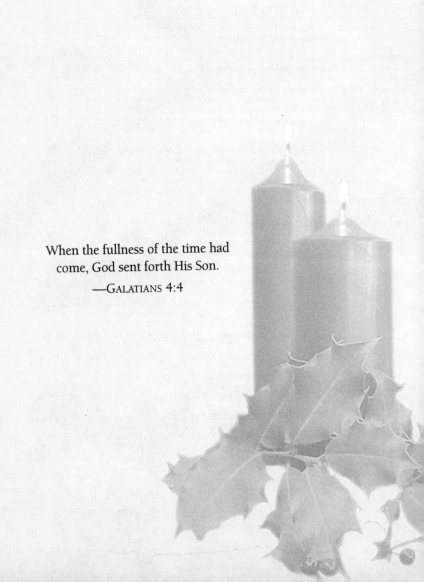

When the fullness of the time had
come, God sent forth His Son.

—GALATIANS 4:4

The Simple Beginning

This story happened once upon a time. But it is a true story and not a fairy tale, myth, old wives' tale, or figment of someone's imagination. The characters are not simply one-dimensional stick figures. They are human beings made of flesh and blood, with feelings, struggles, hopes, and dreams similar to our own. They are real people like you and me.

All of them, except for one, had something very important in common. And that is that they were each visited by an angel of the Lord and given revelation as to the part they had been called to play in the dramatic unfolding and fulfillment of the greatest promise God had ever given to His people. Even though this story took place more than two thousand years ago, there is something in every part of it, and in each person involved, that speaks powerfully to us right where we live our lives today.

The story of the birth of Jesus usually sits on a shelf for most of the year. We bring it out in December, dust it off, let it shine for a few weeks, and then pack it up shortly after Christmas and put it away for another 11 months. But this wonderful story has meaning for every day of our lives. It is a message of hope that says God always remembers His promises and fulfills them in His perfect timing. It tells us that God uses ordinary people who love Him to do extraordinary things for His kingdom. It encourages us to believe that God can birth something great in us, even when we know there is no possibility of that ever happening on our own. It assures us that with God, nothing is impossible. It reminds us that God loved us enough to send His own Son—part of Himself—to be with us as a light in the midst of our darkness, and a hope in the center of our hopelessness, in order to bring us into an abiding walk with Him. May I suggest that this is a story for all seasons.

Chapter One
The Unbroken Promise

A long time before this story ever took place, God revealed important pieces of it to some of His prophets. He told them a day would come when His own Son would be born on the earth. Three of the most important of these prophets were Isaiah, Micah, and Jeremiah.

*I*f you were to compare each of God's prophets to a musical instrument, *Isaiah had a voice like a trumpet.* It rose strong and clear across a wilderness of godlessness. It was a voice both cacophonous and melodic, depending on who was listening. It became God's instrument, used to proclaim. To announce. To warn. And its sound wafted in the air long after the trumpeter had ceased to play.

"God's displeasure with your evil, rebellious, corrupt, and idolatrous ways will bring His judgment upon you," declared Isaiah in a voice of unwavering strength to the people of Judah.

"Be quiet, Isaiah," said the people. "No one wants to hear this."

"You are an educated and prominent man," said the king of Judah. "You are highly respected for your knowledge of history, economy, and theology. Why don't you stick with what you know? You and I enjoy a close relationship, Isaiah. Why do you strain it with these depressing predictions?"

"It's because I have a close relationship with God that I must tell you whatever I hear from Him," Isaiah replied.

In the midst of Isaiah's prophecy of gloom, however, came a message of hope.

"God will bring a way of redemption to those with a humble and repentant heart," Isaiah said. "The Lord Himself will give you a sign. The virgin shall conceive and she will bear a Son, whose name shall be called Immanuel."

Isaiah went on to explain that this Child, Immanuel, which means "God with us," would be a righteous King who would rule the earth forever.

"His name will be Wonderful, Counselor, Mighty God, Everlasting Father, Prince of Peace," he proclaimed.

Everyone liked this part of the message, but *they didn't have hearts that were humble or repentant enough to receive it.*

Micah had a voice like a timpani. It pounded out the beat of God's will. Percussive, penetrating, noisy, and irritating to those who did not want to march to it. Clear, precise, rich, and majestically compelling to those who had a heart to follow.

"God's judgment is coming upon you!" Micah warned the people of Judah and Israel. "You people covet things and are rebellious. You have contempt for God's Word and you worship false gods. You rich people are oppressing the poor. You rulers do not uphold justice. You will surely fall to your enemies unless you repent!"

"You're too extreme, Micah," said the people. "You speak well, but you never say anything nice."

"Calm down, Micah," said the king. "Don't you think you're taking your job a little too seriously?"

In the midst of Micah's prophecy of doom, however, came another message of hope.

"The Lord has spoken to me about you, Bethlehem," declared Micah to the people. "You are the least significant town in all of Judah, yet out of you shall come the most important Ruler in Israel. He will feed His flock like a good shepherd, and all who follow Him will dwell securely. He will rule forever and bring peace to anyone who receives Him."

Everyone liked this part of the message, but *they didn't want to obey God.* They wanted to follow their own desires and dreams instead of doing what God was requiring them to do.

Jeremiah had a voice like a solo violin. It soared above the din of all concerted efforts against him. Its lyrical sound deeply penetrated the righteous souls who would listen, filling them with sorrow and mourning for the sins of their nation. To the godless, however, his voice was interminable shrieking that had to be silenced. So they isolated it by ridicule and rendered it solitary by persecution.

"You rulers are corrupt, but you religious leaders are even worse," declared Jeremiah to the people of Judah and Israel. "You are the ones who are supposed to hear God's voice, and yet you are sold out to your own selfish ambitions. I despise your idolatry. I am grieved that you disregard the laws of God. If you do not change your ways, you can be sure that God will deliver you to your enemies."

"Quiet, Jeremiah!" said the people. "Stop talking about coming disaster. We want to hear something positive."

"I don't believe you really hear from God," said the king to Jeremiah. "Therefore your predictions that we will be taken into exile by our enemies amount to treason. Your writings must be destroyed!"

The king's fury prevailed. Jeremiah was unfairly convicted of treason and his writings were publicly burned. But nothing could destroy the anointing of God upon him, so he lived to write the same words again. This time with a message of hope.

"The days are coming when God will raise up a branch of righteousness from the house and line of King David," declared Jeremiah. "This King will reign forever and save His people from all of their enemies."

Everyone liked this part of the message, but *they didn't have enough faith to believe it.*

The people did not listen to God's prophets, and so exactly as Isaiah, Micah, and Jeremiah had warned, Israel and Judah were captured by their enemies and fell into the hands of cruel and oppressive rulers. Then the voice of all prophecy ceased.

It would be four hundred years before any prophetic voice was heard again.

For four centuries people remembered what the prophets had said. All their prophecies of doom had come to pass. Surely their prophecies of hope would, too. God had promised to send His Son to redeem them, so they watched for the Messiah to come. They looked for His light to penetrate the darkness of their existence. They thirsted for His living water in their dry and barren lives. They yearned for a Deliverer to set them free from their oppressors. They desperately needed His everlasting peace to invade their endless unrest. They cried out to God to send the Savior. He was their only hope.

Into the midst of this dark, hopeless, watching, yearning world, our story begins.

My Prayer to God

Lord, thank You for speaking to us through Your Word and Your prophets. It strengthens my faith to read of the many things that were prophesied in Your Word which have already come to pass. I know this means that *every* promise in Your Word will be fulfilled. Thank You for always keeping Your promises. I pray that I will not be like the people in Isaiah's time who would not *humble* themselves before You and listen. And I don't want to be like the people Micah spoke to who refused to *obey* You. Nor do I want to be like the people who heard Jeremiah's prophecy but didn't have *faith* enough to believe it. Instead, I humble myself before You this day and ask that You would help me to clearly hear and understand Your instructions to me. Enable me to fully know Your laws and obey them. Give me ever-increasing faith to believe that Your promises are true. Help me to see all the promises to me in Your Word so that I can claim them, stand strong in them, and rest in You as I wait for them to be fulfilled in my life.

In Jesus' name I pray. Amen.

God's Promise to Me

Faith comes by hearing,
and hearing by the word of God.

—ROMANS 10:17

Chapter Two
The Surprise Visitor

The story began in Jerusalem during the days when a very wicked king, Herod the Great, was on the throne. The Herods were a ruling family known for their cruelty, and Herod the Great was the worst of them all. Even though he brought order and economic stability to Palestine, he still ruled as a tyrant who put fear in the hearts of anyone remotely close to him, including his own family. But he was nothing more than a pawn of the Roman government, which was even more oppressive and heartless than he was.

*H*erod was called "the Great" because he loved to build. It was one of the ways he strived to secure his own immortality. And so he built many cities and heathen temples. He even took it upon himself to rebuild the Jewish Temple in Jerusalem in order to gain favor with the religious Jews. He thought he could win over *both* the Jews and the Roman officials by not only restoring the Temple, but also by making it impressively bigger and more beautiful. In order to do that, Herod had to assure the Jewish religious leaders that he would not interrupt any of their Temple activities.

The only men ever allowed to enter certain parts of the Temple were the priests. Not even Herod's builders were permitted to go into those places. King David had divided the priests into 24 groups centuries earlier, and the eighth group could trace its line back to Aaron. Now one of Aaron's descendants, Abijah, headed the division of priests to which an elderly man named Zacharias belonged.

This was Zacharias' week to serve at the Temple. He had arrived on the Sabbath and was to stay in the Temple until the following Sabbath. He always looked forward to this week because he believed his priestly duties were a divine calling, a fulfilling of God's will for his life.

On this particular day, Zacharias had been chosen by lot to burn incense in the Holy Place. His duties as a priest were to be in charge of sacrifices and offerings at the altar, to lead worship in the shrine, to teach people the law of God, and to help them determine God's will. The highest privilege of all was to be chosen to burn incense in the Holy Place. It was something a priest would do only once in a lifetime, and some priests never did it at all. Zacharias had often wondered if he would ever be chosen for this privilege, and now that great day had arrived.

"Thank You, God, for this opportunity to serve You in the highest capacity possible," Zacharias prayed with humble excitement as he put together the specific mixture of aromatic spices to make up the incense. He thought of how thrilled his wife, Elizabeth, would be when he returned home at the end of the week and told her of this wonderful honor.

Zacharias and Elizabeth had been married for more than half a century, but much to their disappointment they were never able to have any children. Elizabeth was barren. For years they had prayed daily for a child, until it finally became obvious that God was not going to bless them in that way. Now Elizabeth was well beyond childbearing years, so they had long ago stopped thinking that having a baby would ever be a possibility for them. Instead, they put all their energies into serving the Lord.

Elizabeth will want to know everything about this, thought Zacharias, as he took fire from the altar of burnt offering and brought it into the inner room of the sanctuary, placing it on the altar of incense. *I must remember each detail so I can tell her.*

Zacharias noticed the beauty of the altar, which was built of the finest acacia wood and overlaid with pure gold. He wanted to touch it, but he knew he mustn't because it was next to the Holy of Holies. The very presence of God was in the Holy of Holies. That's why it was separated from the rest of the Temple by a veil-like curtain. He knew he must be careful to do everything exactly as he had been instructed, and nothing more.

As was the custom, when Zacharias entered the Holy Place, the people immediately left the Temple to gather outside and pray. They were supposed to continue praying there until he came out to speak a blessing over them. With the people gone, he became very aware of the silence.

Carefully holding the gold vessel that contained the incense, Zacharias poured it slowly on the fire. As the incense burned, it enveloped the area in a fragrant smoke that he hoped would be pleasing to God. As he began to bow with great reverence toward the Holy of Holies, there suddenly stood before him on the right side of the altar of incense a being having the appearance of a man. Zacharias jumped slightly, for it was quite startling.

Certainly no man would be allowed to enter into this area of the Temple without being stopped, thought Zacharias. *And in the silence of this room, I would surely have heard someone coming in.*

But this visitor was no ordinary man. He was larger than life, not so much in his size as in the glory that was unmistakably upon him. He was surrounded by light, and it appeared to shine both through him and from him.

Is this an angel? Zacharias wondered. *But he has no wings like cherubim and seraphim do. He is different.*

The presence of this being took Zacharias' breath away. Greatly troubled and nearly paralyzed by fear, he was about to fall forward on his face when the angelic being spoke.

"Do not be afraid, Zacharias," the angel's full, rich voice penetrated deeply into Zacharias' soul. "Your prayer has been heard."

Which prayer? thought Zacharias as he silently searched his memory. Immediately his unspoken question was answered.

"Your wife, Elizabeth, will conceive and bear a son, and you shall call his name John," said the angel. "And you will have joy and gladness, and many will rejoice at his birth."

Zacharias put his hand over his heart and tried to breathe. He felt almost as if he were going to faint. This news was too great to comprehend.

Dare I believe it? Is this really happening? Or is this just a day-dream of my own imagining? Zacharias wondered to himself.

"He will be great in the sight of the Lord," the angel went on, describing the son that Zacharias and Elizabeth would have. "But he must not drink any wine or strong drink, for he is to be set apart to God. He will be filled with the Holy Spirit from the time he is in his mother's womb. He will turn many of the children of Israel to the Lord their God."

Zacharias silently struggled to take it all in.

"He will go before the Messiah in the spirit and power of Elijah," continued the angel, "to turn the hearts of the fathers to the children. He will prepare the people for the coming of the Lord."

The Messiah? The coming of the Lord? A son to prepare the way? Zacharias' mind raced. *How can I be certain? How can I know for sure that this thing I've prayed a lifetime for is really coming true? Is this just wishful thinking? The vain thoughts of a desperate man? I want to believe, but I'm afraid to hope again. Can it be that I will know an answer to this hope I've carried so long within me?*

The thoughts that swept over Zacharias in an instant also brought a flood of tears. He choked them back, but several escaped down his cheeks, and he silently caught them with the back of his hand.

"How shall I know this is true?" he asked the angel, unable to contain his questions any longer. "For I am an old man. And my wife is old, too."

The angel appeared to stand up even taller and more majestic than before, and his voice became deeper and stronger.

"I am Gabriel, who stands in the presence of God, and I was sent to bring you this good news."

Gabriel? Sent by God to me? The thoughts in Zacharias' mind raced like a whirlwind, sweeping his strength away. He nearly stopped breathing.

"Because you did not believe my words," Gabriel's voice thundered, "you will not be able to speak again until the day these things I have told you take place."

Immediately Gabriel vanished and Zacharias was left in a deafening silence. Time seemed to stand still as he contemplated each word he had just heard. Still visibly shaken, he slowly returned to his tasks at the altar of incense.

The crowd of people who had gathered outside to pray grew increasingly restless as time went on. Having been kept waiting far longer than they expected for Zacharias to appear, they now began to talk among themselves.

"What's keeping Zacharias, the priest?" asked Jacob.

"Zacharias?" questioned Joshua.

"Yes," answered Nathaniel, "he was the one chosen today to offer incense."

"What a shame he and Elizabeth never had any children," whispered Deborah.

"I don't think it was because God was displeased with them," answered Naomi.

"No, they're such a nice couple," added Martha.

"Why is he taking so long?" asked Simon impatiently.

"It's getting late," worried Rachel. "We really need to be going."

"Well, we can't leave until he pronounces the blessing," Joshua reminded her.

At that moment Zacharias came out of the inner sanctuary and walked slowly to where the people were gathered.

"Wait, I see him!" shouted Rachel.

"Here he comes," called Nathaniel.

"Shh!" commanded Jacob. "He is going to pronounce the blessing."

Zacharias raised his hands to silence the worshipers, and they quieted immediately. He moved his lips as if to speak, but no sound came out of his mouth. It startled him, and he immediately brought his hand up to his throat. Swallowing hard, he remembered what Gabriel had said and recognized this as the predicted sign. Just to be certain, he tried again to speak, this time with even greater effort. But still he could not utter a sound. The people stared dumbfounded at him.

"Why isn't he saying anything?" questioned Deborah.

"He's trying to speak," said Nathaniel, "but he's not making a sound."

"What's the matter with him?" inquired Joshua.

"Is he all right?" asked Rachel.

"What is it, Zacharias?" called out Simon.

"Tell us with your hands," suggested Naomi.

Zacharias gestured in an attempt to describe what had happened, but still the people couldn't understand.

"What is he trying to say?" asked Martha.

"I think he has seen something," replied Simon.

"Was it a vision, Zacharias?"

"Was it an angel?"

"Was it *God?*"

Zacharias nodded yes, and everyone gasped in astonishment as they tried to imagine what possible reason God could have to render the priest speechless.

"Zacharias has heard from God!" declared Naomi, her voice filled with wonder and fear.

Turning slowly around, Zacharias went back inside the Temple as the crowd stared in silence. When he was out of sight, they quickly dispersed with a rumble of low murmurs and one question on their mind.

What on earth is God doing?

My Prayer to God

Lord, I thank You that You always hear the prayers of Your people who are humble in heart. Even when the answer seems so long in coming, I know that doesn't mean it won't come at all. It just means that Your timing is perfect and we need to trust it. Help me to be patient as I wait on You for the answers to my prayers. Help me to wholeheartedly accept the timing and the way in which Your answers come. Thank You that just as Zacharias was in the midst of faithfully serving You when his greatest blessing occurred, I, too, can simply trust that as I serve You faithfully, You will bless me with all You have for me. I know that no matter how impossible things may seem, all things are possible with You. I am sorry for anytime I have doubted that. Forgive me for ever questioning the great things You are about to do in my life. Help me to always have faith that at any moment—even when I least expect it—You can do a miracle in my life.

In Jesus' name I pray. Amen.

God's Promise to Me

He does not forget the cry of the humble.

—PSALM 9:12

Chapter Three
The Impossible Dream

Zacharias finished up the last few days of his week of priestly duties and then set out southward from Jerusalem to travel the 19 miles home to Hebron as quickly as he could. The entire Temple had been in a complete stir over his inability to speak, and he was eager to leave and not have to attempt any more explanations. Besides, he could hardly wait to tell Elizabeth what had transpired with Gabriel. He was anxious to see her face when she read the letter he had written for her. How he wished he could speak. It would be so much easier to explain everything that way.

"Why did I ask Gabriel for a sign?" he mentally flogged himself. "Wasn't the appearance of an angel from God sign enough? But then again, this is part of the proof. My not being able to speak means that it is happening just like Gabriel said it would."

*E*lizabeth rose from her bed earlier than usual on this morning. She had much to do. Zacharias was coming back, and she wanted their home to have the fragrance of a fresh cleaning, newly baked bread, and Zacharias' favorite stew. As she chopped with her knife vigorously up and down on the vegetables she had purchased the day before at the marketplace, she thought of how good it would be to have her husband home again. She missed him more than ever this time.

Zacharias was her life. Without children to occupy her time, she devoted most of it to taking care of her husband and their home. Of course, she also served God in whatever capacity she could. She, too, was a descendant of Aaron, and it was considered commendable for priests to marry within their own family line so that the priesthood would remain pure. But being a woman, Elizabeth could not serve as a priest. So she served the priest God had given to her.

Zacharias and Elizabeth had always tried to walk in a righteous and holy manner, diligently keeping the commandments of the Lord. As a result, they both knew that her barren condition was not the result of sin. And so they did not allow this great disappointment to cloud their joy. Certainly they had shed many tears over it, and they continued to feel their loss, but they were not bitter. They put their energy into serving God and caring for others. As a result, they were loved by everyone who knew them.

As a woman, however, Elizabeth knew that being child-less was looked upon by many as a curse. Some people even believed that barrenness meant God had withdrawn His favor. This reproach was difficult for Elizabeth to endure. But even more than that, not being able to raise her own child, and never having a son to carry on the family name or be a comfort to her and Zacharias in their old age, was always a hard reality. When Elizabeth finally let go of that burning desire for a child, it was as if she had experienced a death. Laid to rest years ago, it was an impossible dream now.

Elizabeth placed the hot bread on a cooling board and stirred the lentil stew. Zacharias was not due to arrive until sundown, which was at least another hour away. So she had her back to the door when it burst open and flooded the main room of their small house with light. She turned quickly to see who was there.

"Zacharias, you're home already?" she beamed happily as she laid down her wooden spoon and walked quickly to him with her arms outstretched. She hugged him and took the cloak from his shoulders, hanging it on a hook next to the door. Immediately she sensed that something was different.

"What is the matter, Zacharias? What is this strange new look in your eyes?" she questioned. "Why don't you speak?"

Zacharias pulled from his pocket the rolled-up piece of papyrus upon which he had written his letter and handed it to Elizabeth.

"A letter for me?" she exclaimed as she unrolled the top of it. "From you?" She looked up at him incredulously. "What does all of this mean?"

He gestured for her to sit down, which she did, and he took a seat next to her. She read silently for a moment and then looked up at him suddenly.

"A son? For us?" she exclaimed. "But we are…well… we're old."

Zacharias motioned for her to continue on. She read more quickly over his words and when she looked up again, tears spilled from her eyes and watered her cheeks in limitless measure.

"I've dreamed of giving you a son, Zacharias," she said softly. "And I thought I saw the death of that dream. But I do trust that all you've heard and seen are from God."

Zacharias put his hand on her arm and smiled. He thought of being with Elizabeth again in that same closeness they had known for years, but now with the hope and anticipation they had shared when they were young. It was almost too much happiness for him to endure.

Even if I could speak, I don't think I would in this moment, thought Zacharias. He struggled to control his own tears, but they came streaming down his face. He began to have thoughts he had not allowed himself to have for many years.

"Deep in my heart there was always this ember of longing," said Elizabeth, drying her tears with her apron. "I guess it was kept warm by the flame of my own desire. It was a dream I held in secret, even though I yearned to hold it openly. It was fanned by my hope into a fire that burned to such heat I could no longer touch it. So I extinguished all that would keep it alive. I never told you, Zacharias, but that dream never died."

Zacharias caressed her hand and smiled.

"Oh, Zacharias, isn't it just like the Lord to invite us to put our dreams into His hands? Asking us to release our grip on them, to forever surrender our plans? And then, when He's certain it's not born of men, He calls for that fire to rekindle again. And He asks us to know with our hearts what we can't see with our eyes. It must be God when our dream never dies."

Zacharias nodded with full understanding. He took Elizabeth in his arms and embraced her tightly. She was as beautiful to him then as she had been as a young bride.

Within a few weeks, Elizabeth was certain she had conceived. She and Zacharias determined they would not say anything about this to anyone until it could no longer be hidden. They found, however, that although her condition could be concealed, their joy could not. They couldn't stop thanking God for bringing this new life where there had been no possibility of it before.

"The Lord has done this for me," Elizabeth marveled time and again. "He has looked on me kindly and heard all my prayers. He has taken away my shame, and I will no longer be looked upon as an object of pity. I thought my life was nearly over, and now I have a future I didn't think possible. And this child is a sign that the Messiah is coming. God has kept His promise."

Unable to disguise her emotions, Elizabeth's happiness overflowed noticeably in public.

"What has gotten into you, Elizabeth?" people often said when they saw her.

If you only knew, she thought and smiled broadly at them.

My Prayer to God

Lord, like Elizabeth, I, too, have a dream that has not been fulfilled in my life. I surrender that dream to You, because if it is not of You I want You to take it out of my mind and my heart. Remove from me all longing for it. If it is a dream of my own making, replace it with the dream *You* want me to have. I only want *Your* will to be done in my life. But if this dream I have is one that *You* have put within my soul, I pray that You will bring it to pass. I know that the desires of my heart can't happen without Your power and Your touch. I also know that dreams don't come to fruition overnight and that You have a purpose in the process. Help me to be patient to wait on You and not be tempted to run ahead in order to make something happen on my own. Help me to have faith in the fulfillment of Your promises for me, even during the times when I can't see anything of the possibility of it ever happening. Enable me to know in my heart all that I can't see with my eyes so that dream in me never dies.

In Jesus' name I pray. Amen.

God's Promise to Me

With God nothing will be impossible.

—LUKE 1:37

Chapter Four
The Secret Miracle

Quite some distance north of Jerusalem, between the Jordan River and the Mediterranean Sea in the region of Galilee, there was a small town nestled in the hills called Nazareth. In this remote, uncultured village of little prominence, a young girl named Mary lived in a small, modest home with her family. She was a relative of Elizabeth's, but because of the distance between their towns, she had not seen Elizabeth more than a few times in her life.

*M*ary was a young woman of strong faith, graced with a quiet and humble spirit far beyond her 15 years. Her deep love for God and knowledge of His Word were very unusual for a girl her age. But her father had often read the Scriptures to her and taught her the history of their people. He wanted her to know that even though their family was neither wealthy nor esteemed, they had descended from the royal line of King David and had known great honor and riches in the distant past. Her father had carefully kept their genealogies, and so Mary knew that the man she was engaged to marry was someone from the same royal line as her own. He was a carpenter named Joseph.

Mary's engagement, like other engagements of the day, was a formal agreement initiated by Joseph's father with Mary's father. Once the written agreement had been drawn up between the two fathers and the dowry exchanged, the couple was legally and officially engaged. This contract was as binding as marriage and could not be reversed except through divorce. So Mary and Joseph were considered husband and wife, even though they would not live together or consummate the marriage until after the wedding ceremony took place.

On this particular day, Mary finished drying the dinner dishes and put them carefully away as she always did. She said goodnight to her mother and father and went into her room to get ready for bed. After she laid out her bedclothes and kneeled down to pray, the room was suddenly filled with light. She quickly looked up to see that the source of that light was coming from a being of breathtaking stature. Although she did not know for certain who he was, she sensed a presence about him far beyond that of any normal man. Mary was startled and greatly troubled at his appearance.

"Rejoice, highly favored one," Gabriel said. "The Lord is with you. Blessed are you among women."

Mary was speechless with fright. *Who is this? And what is he talking about?* she thought to herself. *He must be a messenger, but why is he coming to me? Men do not come to women like this. But then he is more than a man. He is like an angel.*

"Do not be afraid, Mary, for you have found favor with God," Gabriel continued. "You will conceive and bring forth a Son, and you shall call His name Jesus. He will be called the Son of the Highest. The Lord will give Him David's throne, and He will reign over the house of Jacob forever. There will be no end to His Kingdom."

Joseph is a descendant of David, Mary thought quickly to herself, *but I'm not going to be married to Joseph for some time. Son of the Highest? David's throne? That means God's Son is coming to reign over Israel just like God promised in the Scriptures.*

"How can this be, since I do not have intimacy with a man?" Mary said, finally putting a tentative voice to her thoughts. In childlike faith, she was trying to comprehend how this could even be possible.

"The Holy Spirit will come upon you and the power of the Highest will overshadow you," explained Gabriel. "Therefore, the Holy One who is to be born will be called the Son of God."

Mary inhaled silently and put her fingers to her lips. *The Messiah?* Tears formed in her eyes, and she struggled to contain herself. *I am the virgin through whom the Messiah will come?* she thought incredulously. *Why would God choose me to be the mother of our Savior?*

"Elizabeth, your relative, has conceived a son in her old age," Gabriel continued. "She was barren, yet she is now in her sixth month of pregnancy. With God nothing is impossible."

Elizabeth? A son? What a glorious miracle! Mary's heart overflowed with emotion.

"I am a servant of the Lord," she spoke humbly without hesitation. "Let it be to me according to your word."

Gabriel departed and Mary stayed motionless, still on her knees. Then she folded her hands, bowed her head, and closed her eyes.

"Lord, I long to serve You in whatever way You want," she prayed. "I'm just an ordinary girl, yet I am willing to be used as a vessel for You. Holy Spirit, bring forth Your gift of life."

Mary stood up slowly and walked to the small window next to her bed. Gazing out at the sky, she thought she could almost see the face of God.

I must go to Elizabeth and see with my own eyes, she thought. *What a miracle that in her old age she will bring forth new life. But first I must tell Joseph. He must know right away.*

Falling to her knees again, she prayed, "Lord, I have just heard from You, but my soul is still afraid. How will Joseph believe what I tell him? Please prepare his heart."

Tomorrow is the Sabbath, she thought, *and I can see Joseph at the synagogue. I'll ask Father's permission to speak to him alone. I must tell him everything that has happened.*

My Prayer to God

O Lord, I pray You would give me a pure and faithful heart like Mary had. A heart that is immediately willing to believe You and receive all that You have. I know Mary was a holy vessel through whom You did Your greatest miracle on earth. Help me to walk in purity as she did, so I can be holy as You are holy. Enable me to remain free of the world's pollution so that my soul will not be tainted and I can be a vessel for You to dwell in and flow through. Help me to hear You speaking to my heart. Enable me to also understand what You speak to me from Your Word. Whatever You tell me to do, I will do it. Whatever You have for me, I will receive it. I want to serve You in the way I live my life. Work a miracle *in* me and birth something great *through* me. Let it be to me according to Your Word.

In Jesus' name I pray. Amen.

God's Promise to Me

Blessed is she who believed, for there
will be a fulfillment of those things which
were told her from the Lord.

—Luke 1:45

Chapter Five
The Gnawing Question

Joseph sat up in his bed and leaned against the wall of his bedroom. He had been trying to sleep for several hours and couldn't even keep his eyes closed. Ever since he had spoken with Mary that afternoon at the synagogue, he had been deluged with a multitude of emotions. First, there was disbelief. Then shock. Then a combination of sadness, grief, anger, and fear. Even resentment. And now unrest. Everything except unforgiveness. He loved Mary too much to not forgive her.

Joseph had loved Mary for as long as he had known her. He couldn't remember a time when she hadn't been in his heart. Since they had become engaged, his love for her had been released to deepen with no bounds. No matter what she had done, he would always love her. He knew that. Although his feelings for her now were complex, unforgiveness would never be a part of them.

His heart hurt from the news she had given him that day, and he just couldn't make sense of it. When she asked to speak with him in private at the synagogue, he thought it was to talk about their wedding. Then she told him the most unbelievable story. He replayed her words over and over in his mind.

*A*n angel of the Lord appeared to me," Mary explained softly. "He said that the Holy Spirit will come upon me and I will conceive. He said I will give birth to a boy and He will be God's Son—the promised Messiah. I know even now that this has already happened."

"Mary, what are you saying?" Joseph responded. "I know the Scriptures promise that the Messiah will be born on earth one day, but things like this don't just happen to ordinary people like us."

Try as he might, he could not hide his disbelief and lack of trust for what she was saying. He didn't mean to hurt her by his reaction, but he could see in her eyes that he did. Unfortunately, they didn't have much time to talk before she had to return home with her family.

When Mary departed, Joseph's heart was filled with agonizing doubt. It tortured his mind all that day and pained his soul through half the night. He had so many questions, and he was unable to fathom any of the possible answers. One gnawing question—*Is she telling the truth?*—plagued his mind. And now, sitting alone in the darkness of his room with just the moonlight filtering through the small window above his bed, he wrestled with the answer. The torment of it would not let him sleep.

The Mary I know wouldn't do such a thing, he reasoned in his mind. *It's not in her heart to deceive anyone. She could never be with a man who is not her husband. And then to lie about it?*

I'm certain not. Yet there is only one explanation for an unmarried woman expecting a child.

He rubbed his forehead with his fingers and tried to massage away the thoughts.

She said the Child has been conceived by the Holy Spirit, his thoughts persisted. *What am I to believe? Yet, I fear she has betrayed me and been led astray somehow. Did someone entice her? Or force himself on her?* Joseph's anguish rose again and tightened his chest. *My dreams for our future are shattered. How can I marry her now? Even if what she told me is true, how can I marry her?*

He put his head in his hands and prayed, "God, show me what to do. I want to be a fair and just man. I love Mary, and I don't want to make her a public disgrace."

Being a man of high character who was always obedient to the laws of God and government, Joseph was well aware that a betrothed virgin could be stoned to death for adultery. He would never allow that to happen to Mary.

Even if I choose to believe her story, I'm certain no one else will, he thought. *I don't want to expose her for everyone to see. I must protect her from the shame and danger that could come to her when people find out. Of course, there will be some public awareness when I legally unbind us. But I will do this as quietly as possible.*

"Yes," he said to himself. "That's what I'll do. I will quietly draw up the required writings of divorcement and let her save face. But I've thought of her as my wife for so long that it will be hard to think otherwise now. God, help me to do what I must do."

Relieved to have come to a conclusion, although a painful one, the exhaustion of the day overtook Joseph, and he leaned back on his pillow and fell asleep. His slumber was deep and sound, but in the midst of it he had a dream so vivid it was as if he had been awake. In the dream an angel of the Lord appeared to him, full of light and accompanied by the awesome presence of God's glory.

"Joseph, son of David," said the angel, "do not be afraid to take Mary as your wife. For that which is conceived in her is of the Holy Spirit. She will give birth to a Son, and you shall call His name Jesus. And He will save His people from their sins."

When the angel was gone and the dream ended, Joseph woke with such a start he had trouble breathing at first. Gasping, he sat up suddenly. He could remember every detail of the vivid dream and each word spoken by the angel. The awesome sense of God's presence he had felt in the dream still permeated the dark room. Immediately words came to his mind that he had heard spoken by rabbis in the synagogue as they read from the Scriptures. "Behold, the virgin shall conceive and bear a Son, and shall call His name Immanuel." He got up and went to the window and looked out at the starry night.

"Mary is…the virgin," Joseph said with great wonder, his voice catching in his throat.

"Oh, Lord," he cried, as he fell to his knees beside his bed, "forgive me for doubting her. Forgive me for doubting *You*. I've seen it as in a dream, but I know I have heard from You tonight. It's easy to understand why Mary has found so much favor with You. But that she will fulfill the prophecy of the coming Messiah is…well, it's…it's too great to comprehend."

He wiped the tears from his eyes, but they would not stop flowing. "Thank You, God, that I am no longer troubled and torn. Thank You that I can wed the Mary I love. Thank You for the privilege of caring for her and this Child of Your promise. And I promise You that she will remain a virgin until the Messiah is born."

Joseph, who had been kept awake because of his anguish, now was kept awake because of his joy. He could hardly wait to tell Mary of his dream and what God had spoken to him. How he regretted meeting her happy news with shock, sadness, and disbelief. How it must hurt her still to think he didn't believe what she said. He must seek her forgiveness right away. He must apologize for his inability to comprehend. He could barely endure the short time till sunrise.

I will go to Mary at the earliest possible hour, he thought. *I will ask for permission to speak to her alone. Then I will take her hand and look into her eyes and say, "Mary, forgive me. I didn't understand. I am deeply sorry if it seemed like I didn't trust you. You shared the most glorious news ever to be heard on earth, and I didn't accept your story. I promise to spend the rest of my life making this up to you."*

He lay back on his bed to wait for daybreak, but his mind would not rest. Recalling how his own father had often traced their family lineage back to Abraham, through Isaac, Jacob, Boaz, Ruth, Jesse, and King David, suddenly Joseph was able to put it all together.

I am that descendant of King David spoken of in the Scriptures, he thought to himself in amazement.

"And I am just a simple carpenter," he said softly.

My Prayer to God

Lord, I know You do great things for those who love You. And You do great things through those who live Your way. Help me not to doubt the great things You are doing in my life. When You are bringing one of Your promises to fulfillment in me, help me to see it and have faith. Give me discernment, just as You gave to Joseph, when You speak to me concerning Your will for my future. I don't want to anguish over the things You are bringing to pass just because I don't understand what You are doing. Give me ears to hear, eyes to see, and faith to believe. Forgive me for ever doubting Your ability to make things turn out right. It's so easy for me to think small in relation to what You want to do in my life and not see the bigger picture. I don't want to ever be a hindrance to Your purposes on earth. I want to be Your instrument to accomplish them. I don't want my first reaction to difficult situations, or things that don't go my way, to be that of doubt, discouragement, depression, or fear. Instead I want to trust that You are in charge of my life and will bring good out of everything that happens.

In Jesus' name I pray. Amen.

God's Promise to Me

All things work together for good to those
who love God, to those who are the called
according to His purpose.

—Romans 8:28

Chapter Six
The Joyful Reunion

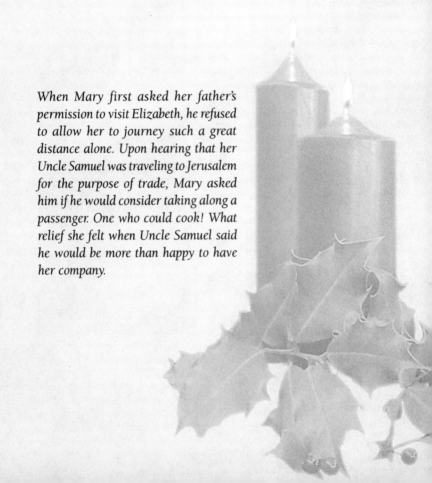

When Mary first asked her father's permission to visit Elizabeth, he refused to allow her to journey such a great distance alone. Upon hearing that her Uncle Samuel was traveling to Jerusalem for the purpose of trade, Mary asked him if he would consider taking along a passenger. One who could cook! What relief she felt when Uncle Samuel said he would be more than happy to have her company.

*B*ut Hebron is nearly 20 miles below Jerusalem, Samuel," said Mary's father. "Wouldn't that be too far out of your way?"

"No, it will be fine," Samuel assured him. "Besides, I have been wanting to stop at the Dead Sea for some time now. A short trip to Engedi will pay for itself. They have the finest dates there, you know, and also balsam for perfume. I can purchase both and easily sell them again to the merchants in Jerusalem along with my other wares."

Mary's father agreed to that arrangement, and so she made plans to leave the following week.

During the long journey to Hebron, Mary had plenty of time to reflect on all that had happened to her. After her conversation with Joseph at the synagogue, when she had given him the amazing news, she had been quite upset. She felt sad and alone that night because she was certain he didn't believe her. How relieved she had been when he came to her home the following morning and apologized. God answered her prayers and revealed the truth to Joseph. She loved him more than ever when he asked forgiveness for doubting her story and then pledged to spend the rest of his life proving to her that he would never doubt her again.

"Thank You, God, for Joseph," said Mary quietly as she bumped along in the back of Uncle Samuel's cart.

She thought about the details of their upcoming wedding. She and Joseph were to be married when she returned, and she was eager for that. She pictured the white robe and veil her mother was making for her. She imagined how Joseph would come to her house, accompanied by his friends along with musicians and singers, and receive her from her parents. Then he would take her back to his house, along with her family, and all their relatives and friends would join together for a wonderful feast. Afterward there would be music and dancing and laughter. Later in the evening her parents would escort her to the nuptial chamber that had been prepared especially for them. Joseph would then come and join her. They planned to sleep together in the same room, but he would not touch her until after the Baby was born. Mary smiled to herself. She knew that Joseph loved her and that she was safe with him.

She knew God loved her, too. From the moment Gabriel appeared to her, Mary had a distinct sense that God's presence was with her and His hand upon her. She didn't understand everything that was happening, but she was certain that God would be with her through it all.

After six days of travel, she and Samuel entered the hill country of Judah near Hebron. Mary felt a rush of excitement knowing that they were getting closer to where Elizabeth and Zacharias lived. Also, she was becoming more and more aware of the new life growing in her. Her whole body felt different. Her joy was uncontainable, and it was hard to not share it with anyone. She couldn't wait to talk to Elizabeth and tell her what had happened. Who else could really understand? And she was eager to see that Elizabeth was now obviously expecting a child. She also had many questions for Zacharias. He probably knew the Scriptures and prophecy better than anyone else. He would be able to explain so much to her.

Samuel steered the oxen cart off the main road and slowly up the hill leading to Elizabeth's house.

"This is close enough, Uncle Samuel," said Mary as they approached the long and winding wide path leading to the front door. "I can see Elizabeth from here. I'll walk the rest of the way. Besides, I know you want to arrive at Engedi before dark."

Samuel pulled the oxen to a halt and turned around to retrieve Mary's bag of belongings from the cart.

"Elizabeth probably won't even recognize me," she said with great excitement as she stood up in the cart and shook the wrinkles from her clothes. "It has been five years since I've seen her. I've changed so much since then."

"Indeed you have," said Uncle Samuel. "Remember, it will be a number of weeks before I come back for you. Are you sure you'll be all right?"

"Oh, yes. Thank you, Uncle Samuel," she said as she leaned forward and kissed him on his cheek. "I can't tell you how much this means to me."

She hopped down from the cart and took the bag from her uncle.

"Goodbye," she called back to him as she ran up the hill as fast as she could.

Through the open front door, she could see Elizabeth sweeping the floor. Without knocking, she peeked her head inside and said, "Elizabeth, it's me. Mary, from your family."

Elizabeth appeared startled at first. She dropped her broom and grabbed her swollen stomach with her hands.

"Mary! Blessed are you among women," Elizabeth greeted her happily. "The mother of my Lord has come to see me!"

"How did you know?" Mary asked with great surprise. "I have not told anyone but Joseph. Only God could have revealed this to you."

"As soon as I heard your greeting, the baby in my womb leaped for joy," explained Elizabeth. "Blessed are you because you believed God. Now all of those things God told you will be fulfilled."

What a relief that Elizabeth already knows! thought Mary as she embraced her cousin. The exhaustion from the journey fell off of her like a silk veil.

"Oh, Elizabeth! Let me tell you what happened," Mary exclaimed with glee. "Gabriel, an angel of the Lord, appeared to me and told me that you had conceived a child. I see it has happened just as he said."

She talked faster and faster, explaining all that the angel had said and how she was now carrying the Messiah within her. The happiness of the moment became so great that she began to speak with a voice full of Holy Spirit-inspired exhilaration.

"My soul magnifies the Lord," Mary's voice rose like a song. "And my spirit rejoices in God my Savior. All generations will call me blessed, now and forevermore."

She grabbed Elizabeth's hands in her own and continued. "For He has regarded my lowly state and He has blessed me for all to see. He's mighty with mercy to those who revere Him. I cannot be silent, I have to praise Him, for He has done a great thing in me."

Mary swung Elizabeth around in a circle, and Elizabeth's voice rose high with laughter.

"He has filled the hungry with every good thing. His mercy extends to all generations," Mary's voice rose and fell. "He has scattered the proud and pulled down the mighty. He has sent help to His people just like He promised. Oh, Elizabeth, I cannot contain my joy."

"Nor can I," laughed Elizabeth, sensing the Holy Spirit's presence like never before as they danced and sang. "I cannot be silent. I have to praise Him, for He has done great things in me."

When they finally fell in a flushed heap upon the large bench next to the door, they laughed to the point of exhaustion.

"Oh, Mary, how did you get here?" Elizabeth asked breathlessly. "And how long can you stay?"

"Uncle Samuel brought me. He's going on to Jerusalem and will be back in a few weeks to take me home so that I can be married to Joseph."

The weeks of Mary's stay turned into three months, but the time passed so quickly it felt as if it nearly flew by. There was much to do to help Elizabeth and Zacharias prepare for their coming son, and of course there were so many things to talk about. Every evening, Elizabeth read from the prophets Isaiah, Micah, Jeremiah, and also from the prophet Malachi, who had foretold of *their own* coming son. It was exhilarating to hear prophecies that were being fulfilled through them. Zacharias and Elizabeth were grateful that in their humble, poor, and obscure lives, God had remembered their prayers and was answering them beyond what they had dared to hope. The happiness the three of them shared was limitless.

Mary had not been eager to get home until the moment she saw Uncle Samuel pulling up the roadway. Then she was excited to go. Even though she loved being with Elizabeth and Zacharias, there were many things to take care of at home. The three of them shared tears and a prayer as they hugged and kissed one another goodbye.

Once Samuel and Mary were on their way, she could hardly wait to see Joseph again. There was so much to tell him. And she was anxious to be married. Even though she was able to hide her condition now, she would feel better with Joseph protecting her from suspicious eyes when it became apparent. She looked forward to the joyous prospect of preparing for the arrival of this precious Child of God's promise. Praise poured out of her heart for all that God was doing.

My Prayer to God

Lord, I can only imagine the joy-filled praise that flowed from Mary's and Elizabeth's hearts as they shared the good news of the coming Messiah. Yet my joy should be even greater because, while they were anticipating the arrival of the Messiah in the future, I have the opportunity to be in Your presence every day. I have Your Holy Spirit in me, and I can come before Your throne in prayer at anytime. Today I come before You in praise. I exalt You, for You are my Lord and King and I am grateful to be Your child. I love You and thank You that You came to earth as my Savior, Healer, Deliverer, and Comforter. I will continually offer the sacrifice of praise to You for I know that in doing so, You are well pleased. May my heart be so full of praise for You that I cannot contain it. May I be so filled with the joy of knowing You that it overflows from me and onto all who see me.

In Jesus' name I pray. Amen.

God's Promise to Me

He who is mighty has done great things for me,
and holy is His name.

—Luke 1:49

Chapter Seven
The Highest Prophet

Soon after Mary left Zacharias' house, it came time for Elizabeth to deliver her baby. With grace in the midst of pain, she brought forth a beautiful baby boy, just as God had promised. Never had the world seen such happiness as that which was found in the eyes of Elizabeth and Zacharias. The love they felt for this child was without limit, and each moment with him became more precious than the next.

When neighbors and relatives heard the news of how God's mercy had blessed Elizabeth and Zacharias with a son in their old age, everyone celebrated with them. Many brought gifts of food and articles of clothing for the baby. The only moment of pause from this daily celebration came with Elizabeth's concern for their advancing years.

"I can't help but wonder how much time God will allow us to have with our son," Elizabeth said privately to Zacharias. "Will I live to see him grow up and fulfill all God has called him to be?"

"I understand your concern, dear wife," wrote Zacharias in response, for he was still unable to speak. "I, too, wonder if I will be able to support him until he is able to support himself. But we cannot allow these concerns to rob us of our happiness now. This child is from God, and God will provide and enable us to raise him up."

*W*hen the baby was eight days old, Elizabeth and Zacharias brought him to be circumcised and officially named, as was the custom. This rite of circumcision was a time of celebration with usually just family members and friends. But because this was such a miraculous and momentous birth and news of it had spread far and wide, there was a sizable crowd wanting to witness it. So, while Zacharias could have conducted this ceremony at home or in the local synagogue, he chose to have it performed at the Temple in Jerusalem. It was a more central location for people to reach, and it was the place where the angel had first appeared to him.

Numerous aunts, uncles, and cousins from the family of Aaron who lived in the areas surrounding Jerusalem flocked to the celebration. And so did the many people who knew Elizabeth and Zacharias because of their long and faithful service in the community and at the Temple. Everyone wanted to be a part of this marvelous event. Clearly, this child was destined to do great things for God. As they gathered from miles around, the air in the Temple was filled with excitement and anticipation. It drew the attention of the townspeople of Jerusalem.

"Why are there so many people gathered here at the Temple?" inquired Naomi, as she entered for morning prayer.

"Zacharias and Elizabeth are having their baby circumcised today," answered Joshua.

"There's Elizabeth!" squealed Rachel.

"Elizabeth, what are you going to name the child?" Deborah called out.

"They are going to call him Zacharias, of course," Simon stated with a voice of authority.

"Yes, everyone knows the child should be named after his father," confirmed Jacob.

"But Elizabeth said they are going to name the child John," insisted Martha.

This statement was so shocking that everyone gasped in astonishment. This was not at all customary, and no one could believe their ears.

"John?" said Joshua in disbelief.

"They're naming him John?" Rachel echoed.

"But there is no one in their family named John," said Simon incredulously.

"Zacharias, tell us what you want to call your son," called out Deborah.

Everyone looked to Zacharias, and several people made signals indicating that they wanted him to write it down. It had been more than nine months since he had last spoken, so no one was expecting him to speak now.

"Here, give him something to write on," said Joshua, extending a tablet toward Naomi, who was standing closest to Zacharias.

"Yes, write the child's name, Zacharias," Naomi said.

She handed him the wax-covered wooden tablet and an implement with which to write. Zacharias carefully carved out the name.

"What does it say?" asked Deborah impatiently, trying to see over Naomi's shoulder.

"It says, 'His name shall be called John,'" answered Naomi slowly.

"John?" Simon asked incredulously.

"John?" echoed Martha.

"They're calling him John?" questioned Jacob.

Everyone began talking at once until Nathaniel raised his hands to silence the crowd. "Shh! Listen! Zacharias can speak again!"

"What? What did he say?" asked Rachel, impatient with the noisy crowd that kept Zacharias from being heard.

"He said, 'Praise be to God for what He has done,'" Nathaniel answered.

"Oh, glory to God!" declared Martha. "The hand of the Lord is surely on him."

"Be quiet, everyone," called out Jacob. "Zacharias is going to speak a blessing over the child."

Zacharias stepped up on a raised platform so all could see him, and he helped Elizabeth up beside him. She was holding their sleeping son.

"The Lord has visited His people as foretold since the world began," declared Zacharias, full of the Holy Spirit. "He mercifully remembered His promise to save us from our enemy's hand."

He took the child from Elizabeth's arms and continued, his voice gaining strength and eloquence. "Now we can serve Him without fear, in holiness all our days. And you, child, will be called the Prophet of the Highest, to go before God and prepare His ways."

There was an audible intake of breath as the people looked at one another incredulously. "This boy is to be God's highest prophet!" they marveled amongst themselves. In their lifetimes they had not heard prophetic words. The voice of prophecy had been silent for hundreds of years. Now Zacharias' prophecy had come to them like a soothing balm, healing the chapped places of their hearts. God was speaking to His people again, and they could not deny His presence. Many began to weep.

"He will call to the hearts of the people. God will instruct him in what to say," Zacharias said as he lifted the child up to the Lord. "He will tell them Messiah, the Savior, is here. He will prepare the way."

"The Messiah?" people whispered with great excitement. "The Messiah is coming? This boy will be God's prophet to prepare the way for the coming Messiah?"

"He will teach to all repentance, and preach forgiveness of sins," Zacharias' voice soared above the crowd. "He will point to the One who will bring us light and peace that never ends."

When Zacharias finished, no one made a sound. They stood silently and let their tears spill unhindered to the ground. The news was grand. It was wonderful. And they believed every word, not only because they had witnessed this miracle child with their own eyes, but also because they clearly sensed the power of the Holy Spirit as Zacharias spoke. It was like nothing they had ever experienced before. They kept their silence until all the details of the ceremony were finished, and then they exploded with praise to God.

From that day on, people talked endlessly about the words Zacharias had spoken over John. They repeated them to all who had not been there to hear it for themselves. And there were many questions. "How will God use this boy to prepare the way for the Messiah?" "When will the Messiah come?" "Has He already been born?" "If He is here, where is He?" "When will He appear?"

No one knew the answers. But they did know that extraordinary things were ahead. They had joyous anticipation that in the darkness of their world, a Light was about to break forth.

My Prayer to God

Lord, I thank You that You are a God of miracles. Nothing strengthens our faith more than witnessing a miracle in our lives. I pray for the miraculous to manifest in me today. And even greater than that would be to pray for a miracle for someone else and see it happen in *their* life. Enable me to do just that. I want to be a part of Your miracle workings here on earth. Just as John the Baptist came to prepare the hearts of the people to receive You, enable me to touch the hearts of others in a miraculous way that will prepare them to receive You, too. I look forward to the day when I can stand in the midst of Your people, just as Zacharias did, and declare that I have seen a miracle with my own eyes. And people will know that the impossible has happened and You have fulfilled one of Your great promises. Thank You that Your Word promises You have so much more for us than we have ever dreamed possible.

In Jesus' name I pray. Amen.

God's Promise to Me

Eye has not seen, nor ear heard,
nor have entered into the heart of man
the things which God has prepared for
those who love Him.

—1 CORINTHIANS 2:9

Chapter Eight
The Royal Decree

In a wedding of simple beauty, exactly as Mary had imagined it would be, she and Joseph were married. As a special surprise, Mary's mother had embroidered her wedding robe with delicate white flowers around the neckline, the edge of the sleeves, and the bottom of the hemline. The embroidery seemed to make the gown glisten as it reflected the light. Joseph noticed it when he came to her house in a procession to escort Mary and her family back to his home.

*Y*ou look radiant!" he said the moment he saw her. "And this gown reflects your beauty."

"Thank you, Joseph," Mary said demurely, casting a grateful smile toward her mother.

After the short wedding ceremony at Joseph's home, the festivities began with a banquet feast. Joseph's family had prepared tender lamb and fresh fish caught that afternoon. There were also vegetables, plums, figs, oranges, pomegranates, and small hollow loaves of bread filled with cheese and olives. The food was simple and delicious and in more abundant supply than anyone had seen for some time. There was even fine wine, which Uncle Samuel had brought from Jerusalem. Happiness was in the air and everyone fell under its power.

Whenever Mary and Joseph caught one another's eye, they exchanged a private smile. Still able to conceal her condition, they continued to keep their precious secret guarded. They decided not to tell their parents until after the wedding was over and they were settled in their new home. They knew that if Joseph himself needed a revelation from God in order to believe Mary, there was no reason to think their parents would be any more inclined to believe her either.

A few weeks after the wedding, Joseph and Mary went to each of their families and told them the entire story. Even though their parents knew about the miracle of John's birth to Elizabeth and Zacharias, it was still difficult for them to readily accept that Mary was the virgin in the Scripture who would give birth to the promised Messiah. However, once the initial shock of it was over, they were thrilled beyond measure.

When Mary's condition could no longer be hidden, other people had to be told as well. But they didn't know what to believe. The news of it spread quickly throughout the town, and it had everyone poring over the Scriptures for weeks. The townspeople argued about it in the public places where they gathered.

"It does say, 'The virgin will conceive' in the Scriptures," said Nahum. "But the Baby is supposed to be born in Bethlehem. This is Nazareth!"

"Jeremiah said that God would raise to David a branch of righteousness," reasoned Jonas. "Mary and Joseph are both from the line of David."

"But they're just…Mary and Joseph. We've known them for years," said Priscilla.

"Yes, shouldn't the mother of the Messiah be…well… more special?" Hannah asked.

"Mary *is* special," said Leah, defending her. "She is not the kind of girl to get herself into trouble, and you know that."

"And Joseph is not the kind of man to marry a girl who would get herself into trouble," argued Jesse.

"It doesn't seem to concern *them*, so perhaps it shouldn't concern *us*," Ruth added.

"Yes, but it does!" said Hannah. "If what they are saying is really true, then it affects all of us. If this Child is really the Messiah as they say He is, then we must be prepared to receive Him."

"And if what they are saying is not true, then Mary is not the girl we think she is," Asher added.

The town was in a buzz over this, in spite of knowing the prophecy Zacharias had given at the Temple regarding his miracle son, John. People debated back and forth, some believing and others not so sure. To certain people there would always be a cloud of suspicion over Mary and Joseph.

The day before the Sabbath was traditionally a very busy market day for the people of Nazareth. All the buying and preparing of food had to be done by early afternoon so that the Sabbath day of rest, which would begin at sundown, could be strictly observed by the Jewish community. The center of town was quite crowded in the late morning on this particular day, when two Roman soldiers and a crier rode in on horseback.

Anytime Roman officials came to town it meant trouble. Usually they were coming to extort money from the people in some way by threatening them if they did not pay a tax. Or they might be wanting to arrest someone on fabricated charges. But if a crier accompanied them, it meant they were there to deliver bad news. A crier never announced anything good.

Almost before anyone could scatter out of the way of the three ominous-looking Romans, they rode swiftly into the middle of the crowd. The crier jumped down from his horse and pulled out a large piece of parchment, which he unrolled as he read in a very loud voice. The townspeople stood silently and listened. When he finished, he nailed it to a wooden post and handed another piece of parchment to Asher, who happened to be the tallest man there. Then the crier quickly mounted his horse and rode off with the two soldiers toward the next town. As soon as they were gone, all the townspeople crowded around the posted parchment to read it for themselves and make certain they had heard correctly.

"Everyone must know of this right away," said Jonas grimly. "We must tell anyone who is not here right now."

"Mary and Joseph aren't here," noticed Nahum. "They must hear of this immediately." Many people nodded in agreement, knowing what the decree would mean for them.

Asher, still holding the rolled parchment, hurried down the street toward Mary and Joseph's house, followed by a number of townspeople. As they approached they could see the young couple working outside in a shaded area. Joseph was sanding a bench and Mary was grinding grain nearby.

"Mary…Joseph…did you hear the news?" Hannah called.

"There has been a decree from Caesar Augustus," declared Nahum.

"It says everyone must be registered," added Ruth.

"The worst part about it is that we all have to go to the city of our origin to do it," Priscilla complained.

"It's outrageous," growled Jonas.

"Does Caesar have any idea the hardship this will be for everyone?" asked Jesse.

"We'll have to travel for weeks," Ruth sighed.

"Cursed be Caesar," barked Leah.

"Quiet!" hissed Asher.

"Silence!" demanded Nahum.

"Do you want to get us into trouble?" Jesse admonished.

"There is nothing we can do. We're helpless against the power of Rome," cried Priscilla with trembling in her voice.

"If only the Messiah would come," lamented Leah.

"Here, Joseph, read it for yourself," Asher said, handing him the decree the crier had given him.

"Joseph, you are from the house and lineage of David…" said Nahum.

"So you will have to go all the way to Bethlehem," Jonas interrupted.

"By the time you arrive, Mary will be ready to deliver her Baby," observed Hannah.

Everyone gasped and looked at Mary. Mary looked to Joseph with questioning eyes.

"Is this true?" she asked him.

"Yes, it's true," Joseph responded.

Without saying anything more, the townspeople scurried off in different directions to report the news to others who had not been in town that morning. Mary and Joseph were left alone as suddenly as they had been invaded.

"What does this mean, Joseph?" Mary asked with great concern.

"It means we must leave right away," he answered. "But first I have to finish a table and both of these benches. We will need the payment I receive for them in order to buy supplies and pay the tax when we arrive."

Seeing the worry on Mary's face, he went to her and pulled her close to his chest.

"Don't worry, Mary," he said, putting his arms around her and stroking her long hair. "We'll take it slowly. We can stop whenever you need to rest."

"How long will we have to stay?" she asked.

"If the Baby is born there, we should remain a week at least," answered Joseph. "But don't worry. We can stay at the inn once we are in Bethlehem."

In the same instant, they pulled apart and looked each other in the eyes.

"Bethlehem!" they both said at the same time.

"The Baby will be born in Bethlehem," whispered Mary, "just as it was foretold in the Scriptures."

They sat down together in silence on the bench Joseph had been sanding minutes earlier. He slipped his arm around Mary's waist.

My Prayer to God

Lord, I know that even when I can't imagine how You could ever bring Your promises to fruition in my life, You have a plan that is beyond my comprehension. I see that often what I think is an inconvenience or hardship is actually part of the fulfillment of that plan. Help me to receive these kinds of things as a blessing and not think of them as a disaster. Help me move into them without complaint, just as Joseph and Mary did. Help me to not fret or worry, but rather to trust that because I am walking with You, these troubles or inconveniences will be for my greatest blessing. Even though You may lead me to a place I never desired to be, I will trust it is the place You have destined for me where I can best fulfill Your purposes. When I am asked to do things I don't want to do, help me to respond the way You would have me to. May my first reaction to these inconvenient changes of my plans be one of rejoicing and willing obedience.

In Jesus' name I pray. Amen.

God's Promise to Me

Let us hold fast the confession
of our hope without wavering,
for He who promised is faithful.

—HEBREWS 10:23

Chapter Nine
The Unexpected Stable

By the end of the week, Mary and Joseph were on their way to Bethlehem. Their donkey, Misha, a wedding gift from Joseph's father, was loaded down with supplies for the journey. In one large basket, Mary had packed two earthen cups, two small bowls, a large metal basin with a handle, a mortar and pestle, a griddle, and a small troughlike bowl for kneading bread. She also brought enough olive oil, herbs, and dried fruit to last until they arrived in Jerusalem and could buy more. In another basket, loaded on Misha's opposite haunch, were some bedding and a change of clothing for each of them. Joseph carefully positioned Mary on top of Misha and made sure she was comfortable and secure. Then he laid three full animal-skin water vessels on Misha's back.

*W*hen they first set eastward out of town, the trip seemed like an adventure. Mary and Joseph talked and laughed and admired the beautiful landscape. The weather was lovely, and it wasn't long before they were at the Sea of Galilee. They found the perfect place to set up their small camp, and so they stopped early enough for Joseph to fish and Mary to enjoy the calm of the setting sun reflecting on the beautiful blue water.

While Mary unpacked the basket of cooking utensils, Joseph unloaded Misha and fed her, and then he set up a place for Mary and himself to sleep. He built a fire and fanned it until it was hot enough for cooking. Mary had kneaded eight loaves of bread before they left on their journey and had kept them moist by covering them with damp cloths. Each night she planned to bake one loaf. On this early evening, as the bread was baking on the iron griddle placed upon the heated rocks that Joseph prepared, Mary chopped the vegetables they bought that day from traders along the way. She cooked them with the small fish that Joseph had caught and seasoned them with the herbs and salt that she brought along. They ate well and went to sleep early.

Rising at dawn the next morning, they finished the bread left over from the night before along with cheese, olives, and dried fruit. Then they packed up everything and were off by the time it was fully daylight. This became their basic daily routine, along with at least two stops during the day to refresh themselves, refill the animal skins with water, and eat another piece or two of dried fruit.

Turning south along the Sea of Galilee, they traveled for about 60 miles to the Jordan River and then followed the river southward for what seemed like forever. There were always people on the road coming and going, but the farther south they went, the more travelers they encountered. By the time they veered westward toward Jericho the roads were crowded. Becoming more travel-weary as the days went on, they spoke less and less so as not to add to their exhaustion.

The six miles to Jericho were long and difficult, but it was an oasis to them when they arrived. The town was sunny and beautiful, and there were lush greenery and palm trees all around. Because wealthy people spent their winters there, many lovely homes graced certain sections of the town. They could even see Herod's winter palace in the distance. Once in Jericho, Joseph purchased balsam to use for medicine. Jericho was famous for it, and he knew they might need it sometime. They also drank from the wells of the natural springs that watered the city and filled their animal skins full of it. The taste was exceptionally refreshing, and even Misha seemed to appreciate it.

They spent that night camped on the outskirts of Jericho, and in the morning they began the dangerous trip to Jerusalem. The hills and mountains on the way were steep and rocky and difficult to navigate. And there were wild animals to watch out for. But it was a breathtaking surprise to see the city suddenly appear over the horizon of the last mountain before they went down into the deep Kidron Valley on the east side.

As they made their way up the final climb into Jerusalem, the weather became cooler. By the time they arrived in the center of the city, Mary was cold and uncomfortable. They decided not to stay any longer than necessary to pick up supplies. Because the decree required many people to be traveling somewhere, it seemed as if everyone was going through Jerusalem to get where they needed to be. The city was dirty, noisy, and crowded, and it was midafternoon by the time Joseph and Mary bought the last of their supplies and were ready to head out of Jerusalem. Wanting to reach Bethlehem before nightfall, Joseph asked one of the local merchants for directions.

"You're headed the right way," said the merchant. "Just keep following that road. It's only about five miles, so you should be able to get there before dark if you don't stop along the way. You and your wife are welcome to take along some water from our well."

"Thank you for your kindness, and may the Lord bless you for it," Joseph said gratefully as he took the animal-skin vessels to the well and filled them.

"I hope you have a place to stay," the merchant added. "I hear Bethlehem is crowded, and they only have one inn, you know. Some local people are renting out spare rooms, but Bethlehem is small, and there are not that many people with homes large enough to have an extra room."

Joseph and Mary exchanged a concerned glance. Joseph thanked the merchant again, and they quickly started out toward Bethlehem. But their travel was slowed, for the road was extremely crowded with travelers coming and going. Everyone wanted to reach his or her destination before dark.

Mary gazed down at Joseph walking beside Misha's head and guiding the animal gently with the bridle. Her husband looked very tired. They had traveled close to a hundred miles in a little more than a week. The journey might have been made in five days had she not been so pregnant that they had to stop again and again to give her relief. Because they had just bought new supplies in Jerusalem and Joseph didn't want to burden the donkey any more than necessary, he carried a large load of them on his own back. Mary observed the strain on Joseph's face. She had never loved him more than at that moment.

Bethlehem was a tiny agricultural village surrounded by grain fields. In the edge of the fields just off the main road, Mary could see many campfires already lit and people gathered around them preparing for the evening meal. She watched them as she rode by and remembered the many nights they had done the same.

Tonight we will sleep in a soft, warm bed at the inn, Mary thought gratefully as she pulled her cloak tightly around her to keep away the chill of the evening air. She felt weary to her bones, and she noticed that Misha seemed to be at her limit of weariness, too. Every step was becoming increasingly labored and painstaking. Occasionally the donkey stumbled slightly, making the ride even more bumpy and uncomfortable for Mary.

When they at last entered Bethlehem, it was nearly dark. Joseph asked a passerby how to find the local inn, and he less than cheerfully gave the directions. They proceeded down the main road a short way and then turned left onto the first side street. The inn was straight ahead of them, nestled up against a hill, and the lights inside looked warm and inviting. Mary felt a surge of relief.

Inside the courtyard of the inn, Joseph tied Misha to a post and carefully lifted Mary down from the animal. He helped her to a bench next to the front door, where she gratefully sat down. Joseph knocked on the front door of the inn, but there was such boisterous commotion going on inside that he wondered if anyone had heard him. He was about to knock again when the door opened.

"Can I help you?" the innkeeper asked gruffly.

"We need a room for the night," said Joseph.

"There's no more room for lodgers," the innkeeper said abruptly without giving Joseph a chance to say anything more. "There is no room left in the whole town. You need to go back to Jerusalem or camp out in the fields outside of town."

He was about to close the door, but Joseph said, "Wait, please. My wife is ready to deliver a baby. We must have some place of protection from the cold night air, some place of privacy and comfort for her. Is there anywhere at all on the grounds? It doesn't have to be much."

The innkeeper directed a brief glance at Mary's burgeoning body and thought for a moment.

"Stay here and I'll see what I can do," he said and shut the door, leaving them to wait outside.

Through the small window, Joseph could see the innkeeper speaking to two young children. They rose quickly and ran out the front door past them, across the courtyard, and into a shed adjacent to the inn that was attached to a cave carved into the side of the hill. Joseph recognized it as a stable where travelers fed and watered their animals and put them up for the night. When the innkeeper didn't return right away, Joseph sat down next to Mary on the bench. He noticed her increasing discomfort, but she did not mention it.

For a brief moment, Mary felt overwhelmed by the inconvenience of these circumstances that were beyond her control.

This trip to someplace she had not desired to go couldn't have come at a worse time. For one instant she felt a great pang of homesickness, her first since they had left, and she wished she were back in her own bed at her parents' house with her mother bringing her soup. But she was also feeling other pangs that concerned her even more. And she had no mother, or any experienced woman for that matter, to ask what these pangs meant.

God, be with me, for I know it won't be much longer, Mary prayed silently. *I don't want to burden Joseph with my complaints. I'll tell him how I am feeling after we are settled at the place I know You have for us, Lord.*

Young Benjamin ran past the two strangers at the front door of the inn and dashed across the courtyard into the stable with his eight-year-old sister, Abigail, following close on his heels. Although Abigail was two years younger than her brother, she could still keep up with him.

"Clean up the straw on the floor," he instructed her with a voice of authority as he handed her a rake and shovel. "Pick up anything dropped there by man or animal and throw it outside in the back."

"Tell me again why we have to clean up this stable," said Abigail. "We just cleaned it this morning, and besides, the cattle don't know the difference."

"Because Dad said we have no more room at the inn," replied Benjamin with little patience. "He thinks we can fit a couple more people in here."

"Who would want to sleep in a stable?" Abigail wondered out loud.

"It's better than nothing," Benjamin responded knowingly as he threw big armloads of clean straw over Abigail's freshly raked areas. He picked up a sack of grain and poured some of it into the feeding trough inside the only vacant animal stall at the far end of the stable.

"Come on, this is good enough," she pleaded. "Let's go. It's cold in here. Besides, here they come."

The children put away their tools and ran out the stable door past Joseph and Mary and their father, who were approaching from across the courtyard. The innkeeper showed Mary and Joseph into the newly cleaned stable and handed them a lantern and four blankets.

"There is water in the well, and you can use that fire in the courtyard to cook if you like," he said. "I have one vacant stall down at the end for your donkey. And my wife says if you need her help, just let her know."

"Thank you," said Joseph gratefully as he paid the man. Then they were alone in the stable.

"The innkeeper apologized, Mary. He said this is all he has. Bethlehem is overflowing tonight."

Mary looked around and spied something in the corner. She walked over to it and knelt down.

"At least we will be safe here. And God is with us, Mary," said Joseph, trying to encourage her. "Everything will be all right."

"Here is a manger," Mary said, running her hand over a big piece of limestone about three feet long and a foot and a half wide. It had been carved out inside to hold food for cattle, but looked as if it had never been used.

Joseph laid down the supplies he was carrying and moved toward the manger to get a closer look.

"It's smooth and clean," Mary continued as she ran her hand over the bottom of it. "We can fill it with straw and put a blanket on top and use it for the Baby's bed."

"I'm sorry, Mary," said Joseph, kneeling down beside her. "We've come so many miles, and I hoped we would find a place of comfort when we came to the end. This is not how I thought it would be. And I can't help but wonder how this can be right."

"It's not the way I thought it would be either, Joseph," said Mary, looking up at him. "I thought that God would make our pathway smooth. Yet I know deep within me that this Child of God's promise will be born in this very place tonight."

"My father told me before we left that the call of God comes with a price and we must be prepared to pay it," said Joseph. "This humble stable must be part of God's plan, too."

"I'm certain of it," agreed Mary, spreading fresh straw evenly in the bottom of the manger. "The glory of the Lord upon us tonight is far greater than we can possibly see, Joseph. I can feel His presence warming this place even now."

She pulled out a small, thick blanket from the inside pocket of her cloak and unfolded it across the straw of the manger. Then she took out a softer and more delicate coverlet and laid it on top. She had brought them all the way from home for this very purpose.

Joseph fluffed the straw on the ground and spread the four large blankets over it for them to sleep on. He helped Mary into a comfortable reclining position on the blankets and then sat down beside her.

"Dear Mary," he said, resting his hand on her head. "You have always been able to see the good in everything."

Mary caressed the Baby in her womb and smiled. She closed her eyes and the smile turned into a grimace for a number of seconds. Then, taking a deeper breath, she looked at Joseph to see the concern on his face as he stared back at her.

"This Child was not *conceived* in the normal way," she said softly. "But I'm certain that He will soon be *delivered* in the manner common to all flesh."

"You rest here, Mary," said Joseph. "I'll unload Misha and put her in the empty stall and pull water for us from the well. Then I'll unpack the cooking basket and prepare something for us to eat."

"I don't think I can eat much of anything right now," Mary responded. "You go ahead. And while you're at it, you'd better get out that little sack of supplies the midwife gave to us."

Joseph took a long, hard look at his wife and swallowed. "God be with us," he said softly. "This Child was promised by God, and by God He will be brought forth."

Mary nodded. "I have never been so sure of anything in my life," she said.

Several hours later, the Child of God's promise was born without incident. Joseph assisted Mary on the birth stool that the innkeeper's wife provided for her. When the Baby was born, Joseph cut the cord and cleaned Him, and Mary wrapped Him in long, narrow strips of cloth, called swaddling clothes, to keep Him protected and warm. Then she enveloped Him in the soft blanket she had brought from home and held Him close to her warm body. She studied His face for a long time while Joseph washed their supplies and put everything away. He was just like any other baby in appearance. Beautiful, bright-eyed, and alert. But there was something deeply peaceful about Him.

"I thought God would make Your pathway smooth," she said softly to Him. "I wanted Your steps on earth to be easy. I wanted You to have a painless and perfect life. But I sense the presence of Your heavenly Father here with us, and He has a far greater purpose for You than I can ever imagine."

Soothed by His mother's voice, the Baby Jesus closed His eyes and fell fast asleep. Mary laid down with Him cuddled next to her on the bed that Joseph had prepared for her. Joseph covered them snugly and then laid down beside them, resting his hand on Mary's shoulder. The three of them slept soundly, and the whole world seemed at peace.

My Prayer to God

Lord, I know that things don't always turn out the way I think they will. I know that just because I am *in* the center of Your will doesn't mean that my path will be easy. And the hard things I go through don't necessarily mean I am *out* of Your will either. During those times when I wonder if the difficulty that is happening in my life can possibly be right, help me to see everything from Your perspective. Help me to trust Your provision for my life, just as Joseph and Mary trusted You in the stable. Help me to persevere and not be dismayed or discouraged. Help me to sense Your presence and not succumb to feeling that You have forsaken me. Help me to trust Your purpose for the uncomfortable things I go through, even though I may not fully understand it at the time. I know that You birth great things in our lives in the midst of pain. Help me to trust that and not waste time doubting or complaining. Help me to see that what I suffer in the moment is nothing compared to the glory that will be revealed in me.

In Jesus' name I pray. Amen.

God's Promise to Me

For our light affliction, which is but for a moment,
is working for us a far more exceeding and
eternal weight of glory, while we do not look at
the things which are seen, but at the things which are
not seen. For the things which are seen are temporary,
but the things which are not seen are eternal.

—2 Corinthians 4:17-18

Chapter Ten
The Birth
Announcement

In the hills outside Bethlehem on the evening of the Child's birth, four shepherds sat around a campfire in an open clearing watching over a large flock of sheep. They had been hired to protect the defenseless lambs from thieves and wild animals, and they did their work with diligence. They were simple God-fearing men who often passed the time complaining about their low station in life and the thanklessness of their profession.

*I*t's cold out tonight in this godforsaken place," grumbled Ezra, the oldest of the four, as he stirred the campfire with a stick. "And we're stuck here with a thousand sheep. While life is exciting everywhere else, the highlight of *our* day is sleep."

The other three shepherds nodded and grunted in agreement.

"Shepherds never make decent money," muttered Daniel, the youngest, as he washed out his dinner bowl in a bucket of water. "We barely earn enough for room and board."

"Nothing ever happens to a shepherd, so you might as well get used to it," responded Zeke, the most lighthearted of the four. "The life of a shepherd is about as boring as can be. While exciting things occur all over the world, nothing ever happens to me."

"Me, either," agreed Ezra.

"Yeah," chimed in the other two.

They sat in silence for a few minutes. Ezra put another log on the fire. Daniel rolled out his bed mat.

"It's lonely out here in this isolated job," complained Jed, the serious one. "Our position is without esteem."

"And we're not exactly every woman's dream," Zeke agreed boisterously, scratching his scruffy beard with one hand and his protruding belly with the other. Daniel and Ezra laughed heartily.

Jed shrugged his shoulders and continued. "Shepherds have a humble purpose. Of our fate…well…few people even care. Sometimes I wonder if God knows we exist."

"If He does, I am certain He's forgotten where," chortled Zeke. Daniel and Ezra rolled on the ground with laughter. Jed resolved not to even acknowledge this outburst of bad taste.

"You're right," Daniel agreed, picking himself up off the ground and sitting down on a log in front of the fire. "Shepherds *are* the lowest of the low. Our lives have no excitement. No great purpose. Except for David killing Goliath, what shepherd has ever gone down in history?"

They each nodded in agreement.

Just as Jed opened his mouth to speak further, they were suddenly surrounded by a brilliant light that appeared even brighter than the noonday sun. In the midst of it a glorious being, having the appearance of a man, stood before them. His visage was so luminous and overwhelming that the four shepherds immediately fell to the ground. The radiance of the heavenly being was so blinding that the shepherds were forced to cover their eyes with their hands. They trembled with fear and were rendered speechless.

This is no ordinary man, thought Ezra. *He must be an angel or a holy messenger of some kind.*

"Do not be afraid, for I bring you good news which will be a great joy to all people," spoke the angel in a voice filled with authority and resonance. "For there is born this day in the city of David, a Savior, who is Christ the Lord. And this will be a sign to you: You will find the Baby wrapped in swaddling cloths, lying in a manger."

One by one the shepherds peered out through their fingers to catch another glimpse of this holy messenger. But as suddenly as he had appeared, countless others similar to him also appeared around him singing a jubilant song of praise. They seemed to float in the air above, with billows of light radiating all around, and their singing was loud, joy-filled, and vibrant.

"Glory to God in the highest," sang the angels over and over in full, rich voices. There came the sound of heavenly music accompanying them, although there were no instruments to be seen. The shepherds were frozen with fright at having this invisible world of the spirit opened up to them.

"And on earth peace, good will toward all women and men," continued the heavenly voices.

When the singing ended, the angels vanished as quickly as they had appeared, and the shepherds were left alone in the dark night. They lay motionless on the ground in a stunned silence until one of them finally spoke.

"Did you see what I saw?" Jed asked cautiously.

"We saw a lot of angels, right?" said Daniel, still trembling.

"Right! Right!" agreed Zeke, Ezra, and Jed.

"Well, what do we do now?" Zeke said. "We can't just sit here."

"If this is the Messiah promised by God in the Scriptures, then we must go to Bethlehem. Tonight!" said Ezra, rising to his feet.

"Yes, let's go to Bethlehem tonight!" demanded Daniel, standing up beside him.

"Tonight? But what about the sheep?" Jed asked.

"Forget the sheep. Let's quickly go," responded Zeke as he pulled Jed up beside him.

"Yes, let's see this thing God spoke to *us*," Ezra said.

"The shepherds!" they agreed in unison. They looked at one another and stood up a little taller.

"God wanted *us* to know," Daniel said in amazement.

The shepherds quickly put out the campfire, gathered their things, and set off toward Bethlehem on foot. All along the way they talked about what had just transpired, and they rehearsed the prophecies concerning the Messiah that they had so often heard and speculated about. They marveled that the angels had appeared to *them*—the least respected and most unimportant of all men. They had not even been in prayer or in the synagogue; they were just doing their job. Of course they *had* been complaining at the time, and that was a little embarrassing. But if this thing proved to be true, it meant God noticed *them*. Perhaps shepherds weren't as obscure and insignificant as they once thought.

"When we get there, how will we find this Child?" asked Jed.

"Don't worry," Zeke answered. "Bethlehem is not that big. How many baby boys could have been born there tonight?"

"And how many of those will be found in a manger?" added Ezra.

"If it's true that the Savior has come," said Daniel, "surely other people will know about it, too."

"Yes, there is probably a crowd of people around Him right now," Zeke added.

"God revealed His birth to us tonight. Surely He will guide us to where He is," assured Ezra.

"Surely He will," they all agreed.

My Prayer to God

Lord, forgive me for anytime I have felt insignificant and wondered if You knew or cared that I exist. Forgive me for ever doubting whether You would hear my prayers or if You would really answer them. For I have found that You do care and You do hear and You do answer. Just as You revealed Yourself to the humble shepherds in Bethlehem, I pray that You would reveal Yourself to me. Just as You led them to a close encounter with You, I pray that You would enable me to see You more closely, too. Because You announced the great news of Jesus' birth to the most humble people on earth, I see that no life is without significance in Your eyes. And no matter how isolated we are, how outcast from society we feel, or how lowly and unworthy we see ourselves, You see us as having value. Thank You that even when I am merely doing the most menial and mundane job, You will meet me right where I am and extend Your love and grace to me.

In Jesus' name I pray. Amen.

God's Promise to Me

God resists the proud,
but gives grace to the humble.

—JAMES 4:6

Chapter Eleven

The Overwhelming Presence

As the shepherds made their way into Bethlehem, they noticed a bright light shining from the sky over a certain section of the town. It appeared to come from a star, but they had never seen such a star before. It had a magnificence that caused the light from it to stream down in rays, the same way sun shines through openings in the clouds after a rain. Out of breath by the time they entered the town, they paused on the main street to survey the situation. The great crowd they expected to be gathered there to celebrate this miraculous event was nowhere to be found. The village was still. The once-busy streets completely deserted. Instinctively they knew to head toward the light shining down from the star.

*T*urning off the main street, they could see that the rays from the star fell over a portion of the inn. Upon entering the courtyard of the inn, they were surprised that the light was directly over the stable. They looked at one another in amazement.

"Can the Child be in there?" asked Daniel incredulously.

"In a stable?" Jed protested. "This surely can't be the place."

"It doesn't seem right," agreed Ezra, "but the angel said we would find the Child in a manger."

"And where else would you find a manger?" chided Zeke.

Although the inn itself was dark and deserted, light could be seen coming through a crack where the stable door had been left ajar. They walked cautiously toward it. They could see nothing through the crack, so they pushed the door slightly open. The light from the star lit up the inside in soft, gentle rays and illuminated a young woman kneeling beside a manger and a man sitting next to her. They knocked on the doorpost and Joseph stood up.

"Come in," Joseph said kindly.

"We have come to worship a Child," explained Ezra.

"Angels revealed His birth to us tonight," Daniel added.

"Tell us, is this where we can find the Messiah we have all been waiting for?" asked Jed.

The shepherds held their breath and stayed close to the door, waiting for Joseph to answer. If he thought they were crazy, they might have to run out of there quickly.

Joseph and Mary exchanged a knowing glance. "God has revealed this to you," Joseph said as he gestured toward the manger. "He is here."

The shepherds let out a sigh of relief. They walked slowly over to where Mary and the Baby were. She extended a welcoming smile to them as she uncovered the Baby slightly so they could see His face. As soon as the shepherds looked upon the face of the sleeping Child in the manger, each one of them fell to his knees. It was more than bowing out of reverence, which they had every intention of doing, but in His presence now they could not stand even if they had wanted to.

"This Child is God," whispered Jed in breathless awe and wonder. "He has come to save us out of our hopelessness."

"He is the promised King who will lead us out of darkness," said Ezra, his face aglow in the light reflected from the Child.

"He is our Lord," Daniel proclaimed. "Our Hope forevermore."

Mary exchanged another knowing glance with Joseph. God sending the shepherds to worship the Child was another sign that they *were* in the right place. Mary had wondered if only she and Joseph could sense the Child's holiness, but as she looked at the rough men prostrate on the ground, she knew these simple shepherds sensed the glory of God upon the Child, too. In the Baby Jesus *was* the presence of God.

The shepherds stayed bowed before the Child, their earlier complaints far from their minds, their dissatisfaction with life no longer in their memory. They were in the presence of God. They knew it. And they needed nothing more.

Tears of joy flowed down their rugged cheeks and praise so swelled up in their hearts that they could not contain it. It overflowed from their lips, gently at first, then with ever-increasing waves of joy.

"This Child is God, and we have come to worship Him," they sang in gentle, rich tones over and over and over, each chorus increasing until it sounded as if they were joined by angels. The sound of their praise was so sweet and pure that it didn't seem possible it could be coming from the same boisterous shepherds who had been heard on the hillside earlier. But then actually these *weren't* the same men. These men had seen the face of God, and they would never be the same.

The thick, safe sense of God's presence in the stable kept the shepherds prostrate before the young Messiah until daybreak. When they finally rose up, they explained to Mary and Joseph all that had transpired with the angels. Mary cherished every word in her heart. Their description of the angel sounded exactly like the one who had appeared to her. And to Joseph in his dream. And to Zacharias. And the star the shepherds had seen over the stable explained the amazing light that had filled the place when the Baby was born. A light like she had never seen before. A light that also brought comfort and warmth to take away the chill of the room.

Will it still be there tonight? she wondered.

By the time the shepherds left, the town was up and busy with morning chores. Unable to contain their excitement, the shepherds enthusiastically shared all that had happened to them with everyone they met. They spoke of it not only to those who wanted to listen, but even to some who did not.

"You're drunk. All of you," some of the people said. "Go home and sleep it off."

"But you don't understand," insisted Zeke. "God has visited us tonight. He has seen our hopeless state and has sent His Son, the promised Messiah. He has not forgotten us. He knew where we were and He revealed Himself to us."

"God revealed Himself to a bunch of shepherds?" people laughed. "Surely not."

Other people, who were acquainted with the shepherds, listened and marveled at their story. "We know these men, and they are not the type to have supernatural visions," they said in their defense.

"But what they are saying is unbelievable," replied the scoffers. "The Messiah born in a *stable*? In a *manger*? Revealed by *angels*? And why did God reveal it to shepherds and not to the chief priests?"

Amid the debate, however, no one could deny that these shepherds seemed radiant. Their faces were luminous, reflecting the glory of God.

And why shouldn't they? They had been in the presence of the Lord.

My Prayer to God

Lord, just as the shepherds discovered in the stable, there is nothing more precious than being in Your presence. I long to dwell in Your presence daily so that I, like them, can reflect Your glory. Thank You for coming to earth as You promised You would. Thank You for making it possible for me to be redeemed and restored. Because of You, my hopeless situation is not hopeless any longer. Because You fulfilled *Your* purpose here on earth, my once-futile life now has purpose, too. I bow before You in awe and gratitude for saving me and giving me an eternal future with You. But until I can see You face-to-face in heaven, I want to know the awesome sense of Your presence in my life that the shepherds felt that night. I want to experience the same transformation that comes with being close to You. I want the kind of joy and peace that was theirs.

In Jesus' name I pray. Amen.

God's Promise to Me

In Your presence is fullness of joy;
at Your right hand are pleasures forevermore.

—PSALM 16:11

Chapter Twelve
The Political Enemy

That same night, east of Bethlehem in the region of Persia, a group of learned men known as Magi observed a star that had never been seen before in the western sky. Because the Magi were experts in astronomy as well as influential men in the Persian government, their opinions were highly respected. Anytime Magi observed a new star in the sky, they believed it was a sign of the birth of an important person in that place where the star was brightest. Because this particular star was more brilliant than any they had ever seen, they were certain that an extraordinary person had been born somewhere in Judea, where this star appeared to be shining.

*E*ven though the Magi, or Wise Men as they were also known, came from a Gentile or pagan background, they had access to the Scriptures through the Hebrew synagogues in their country. Three Magi in particular—Melchior, Balthasar, and Gaspar—were religious scholars and quite knowledgeable about the prophecies of the coming Messiah. They believed that the important person who had been born under this unusual star was the Anointed One foretold by the prophets.

As soon as could be arranged, the three Magi, along with an entourage of attendants, set out to the west on camels. They knew it would be an arduous journey and would take some time because there was no direct or easy route to their destination. Because the land between Persia and Judea was full of barren deserts and rugged mountains, the climate went from miserably hot to bitterly cold. Only men with strong convictions in their hearts would even venture such a trip. These three men felt certain this would be the most important journey of their lives.

The closer they traveled to where the star appeared to be shining down, the clearer it became that it was somewhere near Jerusalem. Having planned to stop there for supplies anyway, they decided they would ask around the city as to the whereabouts of this Child. Surely by this time everyone would know.

When the Magi entered Jerusalem, they created quite a distraction among the people. Even though the city was somewhat cosmopolitan and a major stopover for many traders, few people had seen anything like these three foreigners arrayed in their finery and wealth.

"Can any one of you tell us where we might find the Child who was born King of the Jews?" called out Melchior to the crowd. "We have observed His star in the East and have come to worship Him."

The people looked at one another with trepidation and fear. They whispered among themselves and then stared back at him with expressionless faces. No one dared to answer. Worshiping a new King of the Jews would not be a good topic of discussion in Herod's backyard.

Seeing that their approach was getting them nowhere, the three Wise Men got down from their camels and attempted a more personal appeal.

"Tell me, sir, where can we find the Messiah, who has now been born?" asked Balthasar of one of the merchants. "Surely you know where He is and can help us locate Him."

Again the request was met with silence.

"Not one of you knows?" asked Gaspar incredulously.

The Wise Men continued on through the crowd, making more inquiries, but everywhere they went they were met with the same lack of response.

"Either no one knows anything or else they are afraid to speak," observed Gaspar to the other two Magi.

It wasn't long before the questions of the Wise Men caught the ears of Herod's officials, who immediately took the information back to the king. They were fearful about doing so because it was sure to upset him, but they knew if they didn't say anything about it at all and Herod found out, their lives would be significantly shortened.

"King of the Jews?" Herod roared at the centurion who had been elected to bring him the news. "They're looking for a Child born King of the Jews?"

"Yes, your highness," said the centurion with trepidation.

"You know, of course, that I am half Jewish," said Herod. "And I converted to Judaism at the time I became king."

"Yes, your highness."

"I know the Scriptures well, and everyone in Rome believes they are nothing more than a history book. So I will not tolerate this talk of a newborn King of the Jews. It's preposterous!" Herod pounded his fist on the table next to him.

"I agree, your highness," said the centurion, bravely masking the trembling in his heart.

"I will not tolerate any threat to my throne or my authority, no matter whose Son this Child claims to be. Is that clear?"

"Yes, King Herod. Perfectly clear."

The traumatized centurion remembered that Herod had put to death his favorite wife and his two sons by her. He'd had them killed because he *suspected* they were plotting to overthrow him, even though no real threat was ever proven. How much more easily could he put to death a mere centurion who happened to be in the path of his anger.

"I have been very diplomatic in handling both the Romans and the Jews," Herod continued to rant. "I have made the Romans happy by exacting heavy taxes on the Jews and getting hard labor out of them for Rome's benefit. I have made the Jews happy by rebuilding their Temple without interfering with their religious practices. The Roman Empire is now so big it stretches from Parthia to Britain. It's the empire of the whole earth, and I like to think I had a part in that. Rome rules Judea with an iron hand because of me! Augustus and Antonius themselves, the highest rulers of the Roman government these past years, have made *me* king of Judea, and no one will take that away from me. Do you understand?"

"Yes, your highness. I understand completely," said the centurion, hoping to soon be dismissed from Herod's presence. "What would you like me to do, your highness?"

"I want you to gather all the high priests and religious scholars together in this room within the hour," Herod bellowed. "And I want them to tell me where this Messiah is supposed to be born."

"Yes, your highness," the centurion responded with eager relief. "Right away, your highness." He bowed and backed away from Herod to the door and then left to carry out the king's command.

When the high priests and religious scholars, as well as the political leaders, heard why they were being summoned, they were very troubled. Indeed, all of Jerusalem was troubled. Everyone knew that when Herod felt threatened, heads were sure to roll. And no one could ever anticipate who would be the chosen sacrifice.

The chief priests, religious scholars, and scribes, who were the expert teachers of the law, assembled in Herod's private meeting room and waited nervously for his arrival. The moment he entered, everyone bowed.

"I want you to tell me," said Herod without hesitation, "where the Scriptures say the Christ Child is to be born."

"According to Micah the prophet, the Child is to be born in Bethlehem," said one of the chief priests.

"Yes, it is Bethlehem," everyone agreed. One of the religious scholars read the exact Scripture to him.

This news troubled Herod to the point of desperation. Bethlehem was too close for comfort. Even though this Child couldn't possibly be able to reign over anything for years to come, he still felt insanely threatened by Him. Herod's fear that the Child was an immediate threat to his throne showed clearly in his countenance.

The chief priests, religious scholars, and scribes held their breath. They waited for more questions or one of the insane outbursts Herod was known for, but neither happened. The king dismissed them with no further response. They left the palace quickly, fearing they had not heard the last of this issue.

Herod summoned several of his most trusted men and charged them with finding the Magi and bringing them to his palace to meet with him. As he waited for them, he paced nervously in his meeting room. When their arrival was announced, he put on his royal robe and permitted them to enter. Each of the Magi bowed respectfully.

"King Herod," said Melchior, "we have traveled all the way from Persia to Palestine on an important search and have come to your palace as you requested."

"Thank you, gentlemen," said Herod, impatient to move beyond the small talk and gather the information he wanted. "I understand you've been asking around Jerusalem as to the whereabouts of a Child who was born King of the Jews."

"Yes. We are trained experts on the stars and have observed an unexplainable phenomenon," said Balthasar. "We believe we have seen His star in the East and have followed it to this area. We lost sight of the star when we entered Jerusalem."

"I have asked my chief priests and scholars to look into this," said Herod. "And they informed me that a prophet in the Scriptures reveals the birthplace to be Bethlehem." He studied their faces carefully to see what response this information would invoke.

"If this star is indeed a sign of the Child's whereabouts, then it must be directly over Bethlehem," said Gaspar.

"Go there then," Herod demanded, "and search carefully for this Child. And when you have found Him, bring word back to me."

Sensing the need to better disguise his motives, he quickly added, "That I may come and worship Him also, of course."

"Of course," echoed Melchior with suspicion.

The conversation abruptly ended and the Magi were dismissed. Herod remained alone in the room, pacing the floor like a caged lion.

"These Magi think this Child was born the legitimate heir to my throne. I can see it on their faces. If people begin to believe this, I might be seen as a usurper. I cannot allow it." Herod's paranoia and fear blinded him.

"I'm Herod the King and a friend of Romans and Jews alike," he said loudly. "I'll do what I must to protect my throne. I have a destiny to fulfill and no one can stop me, least of all this Child. This threat! This would-be king! He will have no honor. No one will worship Him."

His mind raced to put together the details of the plan formulating in his mind. He decided that when the Magi returned and told him the whereabouts of this Child, he would have Him destroyed.

Why would these Magi make such a long journey to come and worship a Child unless they believed He is the Messiah?

thought Herod with anger tightening his throat. *And what star did they follow? Why didn't my astrologers see it?*

"Whether these Magi find Him or not," he declared out loud in a fury, "I have devised a foolproof plan from which there will be no way to escape. I'll kill every male child under two, and there will be no Child left to take the throne from me."

Herod collapsed into his large carved wooden chair and let his head fall into his hands. He felt sick with rage. His anger tormented him, but he clung to it with the same vengeance he did his own power. The evil that had been growing in him all these years was now turning him into a madman and slowly destroying him.

"A man's got to do what a man's got to do," he whispered to himself.

My Prayer to God

Lord, I thank You that You came to earth to break the power of the enemy. And that through Your death and resurrection it was accomplished forever. Thank You that You foiled the plans of Satan to destroy the life of Jesus when He was a baby so that Your grand purpose for His life could be fulfilled. Just as Herod's evil plans were foiled, I pray that the enemy's plans for my life will not be successful either. Expose his plans and reveal them to me so that I do not fall into any of his traps. Tear down any stronghold in my life that was erected by the enemy for my demise. Keep me undeceived. Set me free from pride and the deception that comes with it. Deliver me from any wrong thinking. Help me to never stray from the truth. Give me discernment so that I will always be able to distinguish the truth from a lie. Help me to live Your way. Lead me away from all temptation and deliver me from evil.

In Jesus' name I pray. Amen.

God's Promise to Me

The Lord is faithful, who will establish you
and guard you from the evil one.

—2 THESSALONIANS 3:3

Chapter Thirteen
The Public Declaration

The last light of sunset filtered through the small open window in the kitchen area where Mary stood at the table preparing supper. Her Son, Jesus, lay peacefully asleep on a small bed nearby that Joseph had made for Him. She gazed at His beautiful face as she worked. It had been weeks since He had been born, and so much had happened.

*T*hree days after His birth, Mary and Joseph took the baby with them to the authorities in Bethlehem to be registered according to their family line. Not only did they have to give *their* names, but they also had to register *Jesus* as their firstborn son. Now the Roman Empire had it on record that this Child came from the house of King David. At the same time, they were required to pay a tax demonstrating allegiance to Rome. Caesar Augustus wanted to know exactly how many loyal subjects he had, and he was especially curious about the royal line of David. How many of them were there? Did they still believe they were entitled to the throne? She and Joseph did what the law required, but this intense interest in their background concerned Mary.

In the process of taking care of this business, they met a distant cousin from Joseph's family who was also there to register. In conversation with him, Joseph revealed the humble place that provided them with shelter.

"Please come stay with us," said his cousin. "My wife and I have a tiny cottage on our property that is vacant at the moment. You can stay there as long as you like."

Joseph glanced at Mary to see her smile of approval and said, "We would like that very much. We want to stay in Bethlehem longer because the weather is quite cold and we would rather not make such a perilous journey home while the Baby is still so young. We gratefully accept your offer, but only if you will let me make some furniture for you in return for your kindness."

The cousin was delighted with the arrangement and came to the inn that very afternoon to escort them to their new quarters. When Mary and Joseph entered the cottage, they were happy to see it already had a bed, a table, two chairs, and a place to make a warm fire and cook.

A few days later, when Jesus was eight days old, he was circumcised according to Jewish law. The tiny Son of God now bore in His flesh this symbol of obedience. At that same time He was officially named Jesus, just as the angel had instructed Mary before He was conceived.

When Jesus was six weeks old, Mary and Joseph brought Him to the Temple at Jerusalem to present Him to the Lord. They did this out of obedience to the law of God in the Scripture that says all firstborn males are holy to the Lord and are to be set apart for a special purpose. Also, the 40 days of Mary's purification were over, and she was required to offer a young lamb as a burnt offering. Because they were poor and could not afford a lamb, she was permitted to offer a pair of turtledoves instead. When that was completed, she and Joseph entered the Temple court to have the Baby dedicated.

"We are Mary and Joseph of Nazareth," explained Joseph to the priest. "We've come to present our firstborn Child."

Immediately, an elderly man called out from a slight distance.

"Wait! Please wait!" he shouted as he ran up to Mary and Joseph as fast as his frail legs could carry him. He took the Child out of Mary's arms.

"Praise be to God, I recognize Him," said the old man, looking at the face of Jesus. "He is the Holy One."

Tears filled the old man's eyes and spilled down his cheeks as he embraced the Child and looked toward heaven.

"Lord, You are letting me die in peace just as You promised," he prayed. "Today my eyes have seen Your salvation, which You have given to all people. This Child is a light to bring revelation to the Gentiles and glory to the people of Israel."

Joseph and Mary looked at each other in amazement over yet another profound confirmation of who this Child was.

"I'm sorry, let me introduce myself," the old man said to Joseph. "My name is Simeon. For years I have been waiting for the coming of the Messiah, the Consolation of Israel, the One who will save us. The Lord revealed to me that I would not die before I saw Him."

Turning to Mary, he looked directly into her eyes. "This Child is destined for the fall and rising of many in Israel," he said to her. "Though a sword will pierce your soul, you have been entrusted with His care. Through Him hearts will be revealed, and men will speak against Him everywhere."

Mary looked at Joseph with grave concern, and he drew her close to him. They both knew this meant there would be difficult times ahead.

"What my eyes have seen, the Spirit reveals to be the Child of the promise of God," declared Simeon in a loud voice for all to hear. "Though this Promise seems small and fragile, He will be filled with the power of the Lord. Some will receive Him and some will reject Him, but He will never be ignored. He is the Lord."

Mary and Joseph hung on Simeon's every word, and many other people in the Temple stopped what they were doing to listen.

"This Child is the Light of the world, the Savior, Messiah, and King," Simeon continued, his voice full, rich, and warm.

"Now I can depart in peace because of what my eyes have seen."

From across the courtyard the voice of an elderly woman rose up so strongly that it drew the attention of everyone standing around. "Lord, I have seen Your salvation," she declared. "Praise to You, O God, for this blessed Child."

"This is Anna, a prophetess," explained Simeon as the woman made her way to them. "She has not left the Temple in many years. She prays and worships night and day, and you can trust that she hears from God."

Anna's advanced age, plus the depth of her experience and wisdom, were written on her kind and beautiful face. She knew the Scriptures better than any woman, and she had been teaching younger women for years, showing them how to seek God and know His Word. A devoted woman of prayer, Anna strove to honor and serve the Lord in all she did. She had been married only a short seven years before her husband died, and so she had been a widow for decades. Now quite old, she lived at the Temple, dedicating her life to God. Everyone knew Anna, and no one could deny the power of God upon her. She now recognized that God's reward for her years of service had come in this one moment.

"This is the long-awaited Messiah!" Anna announced to everyone in the vicinity, and a crowd quickly gathered. "What my eyes have seen, the Spirit reveals to be the long-awaited Son of God. He is the grand fulfillment of all prophecy. No longer just a distant dream, He has come here to redeem anyone who seeks to know Him."

The people who had gathered around began to praise God with great excitement and many tears.

"He is the Light of the world, the Savior, Messiah, and King," Anna's voice rose above the noise of the crowd. "Now I can depart in peace because of what my eyes have seen."

The singing of praise, the shouts of joy, the unmistakable sense of God's presence in this very public declaration of who this Child was, affected Mary deeply. Anna's and Simeon's words melted over her soul like a soothing balm.

But since that day in the Temple, Mary had not been able to forget Simeon's words. *A sword will pierce your soul,* she heard over and over in her mind.

"O God," she prayed out loud as she gazed at the contented face of her Son sleeping on the small bed. "Protect Him from His enemies. Keep us all safe. Guide us as You always have."

My Prayer to God

Lord, what joy it gives our hearts to know that You sent Your Son to earth just as You promised in Your Word. And because He died and rose again as a sacrifice for our sins, we, like Simeon and Anna, can also die in peace knowing that our eternal future is secure. What hopeless despair we would be living in today had this not happened centuries ago. What darkness we would experience had You not come as You said You would. I see that people who know Your Word and understand Your prophecies and promises are better able to recognize and receive them when they come to pass. Help me to know Your Word so well that I am able to appropriate Your promises for my life. Thank You, Jesus, that You are the fulfillment of all prophecy. Thank You that You will fulfill all prophecy for the future, which means You will return for Your people. I am grateful that one day I will be in heaven with You.

In Jesus' name I pray. Amen.

God's Promise to Me

The wages of sin is death, but the gift of God
is eternal life in Christ Jesus our Lord.

—ROMANS 6:23

Chapter Fourteen
The Wise Move

"Isn't it odd that no one from Herod's court has followed us to see where we are going?" observed Gaspar as the three Magi dismounted their camels in front of a tiny cottage on the outskirts of Bethlehem.

"Yes," agreed Balthasar. "I find it unusual that a king such as Herod would trust three strangers."

"I think it's even more strange that we have come a thousand miles to worship this Child born the Messiah, but His own people are not interested enough to travel five miles to find Him," said Melchior. "The religious scholars who said the Child would be born in Bethlehem have not even attempted to go there themselves."

*T*he star that had led the Magi throughout their journey from Persia, until it became obscure close to Jerusalem, reappeared to them once they were on the road to Bethlehem at sunset. It appeared to travel ahead of them until it stopped directly over a humble cottage. They had come a great and perilous distance to find this Child, and now they were filled with eager anticipation to see Him with their own eyes.

"Good day, gentlemen," said Joseph politely as he stood up from his work in the nearby open shed to greet the Magi.

"My name is Melchior. This is Gaspar and Balthasar. We have come to worship the Child born a King."

"We have followed His star all the way from Persia, and it has led us here to this place," said Balthasar.

"We have brought gifts to present to this Child," said Gaspar. "All we want is to simply gaze upon His face."

"Please come in," said Joseph warmly as he led them to the front door of the cottage and opened it.

"Mary," Joseph called, "God has led these distinguished men all the way from Persia to worship the Child. God has revealed to them who He is." He gave her a knowing smile, which she returned.

"Of course, come in," she said. In light of Simeon's words, she was relieved that these strangers meant no harm.

The Magi approached carefully, but the moment they saw the face of Jesus asleep on the small bed they fell to the floor and worshiped Him. Just like the shepherds, they were so overcome by the presence of God that they were *unable* to stand in His presence. This was no human king. The glory of God on Him rendered the Wise Men prostrate on the ground for some time.

When they were finally able to speak, the Wise Men rose up and took out the gifts they had brought from their country to present to Him. The first gift was gold, recognized everywhere as a precious metal of great worth. The second was frankincense, an expensive, fragrant-smelling incense. The third gift was myrrh, a valuable resin used in perfume and anointing oil. These gifts were commonly given to royalty in their own country.

"Thank you for your generosity, gentlemen," said Joseph, visibly touched. "We are deeply grateful."

"It is *we* who must thank *you*," responded Balthasar.

"We see that into the deep, engulfing darkness of this world has come a Light that cannot grow dim," Melchior said, obviously moved by this experience.

"We know that seekers such as we are will never find the answers they are looking for until they find *Him*," said Balthasar.

"We have tasted all the world has to offer, and we know from experience that it can never fill a heart that is empty or warm a heart that is cold," said Gaspar. "But today the light of this Child's presence has been like a radiant fire, illuminating the shadows of our souls."

"We have seen the Light," Balthasar added. "Now we know His name is Jesus. And darkness will never be the same."

Not wanting to impose upon Mary and Joseph any longer, and having accomplished what they traveled so far to do, the

Magi said goodbye and left the house. Once outside, they discussed their plans.

"We cannot go back to Herod, for he will kill this Child," whispered Melchior.

"Yes," Balthasar agreed. "Surely God has warned us in the dreams we had last night."

"We must travel home by a different way," suggested Gaspar. "Revealing the Child's whereabouts would not be right."

They mounted their animals and left Bethlehem without further delay. But they did not go in the direction of Jerusalem. They went the opposite way and turned off onto a secret route. It was completely dark by then and no one ever knew where they went.

A few days later, Herod discovered that the Magi had left town and did not come to report to him as he had commanded them to do. His fury rose to a new level. They had ignored his wishes in order to protect this new King. This slap in Herod's face produced rage in his heart, and he did not sleep at all that night for planning his revenge. He decided not to retaliate against the Magi, for they were of no consequence to him. He would instead act secretly against the Child before His parents caught wind of his plan and escaped with Him.

Herod summoned a select few of his most trusted, loyal, and cruel soldiers, and ordered them to kill every male child two years old and under in Bethlehem and the surrounding regions. Even though he could nearly pinpoint the time the Child was born within that year, he was not going to take any chances. By killing every male child two and under, he would see to it that there would be no possible way that this Child could survive.

Early the next morning, just before people were to rise from their sleep, Herod's men rode through the entire area and pulled every male child out of bed and slaughtered them one by one. The young mothers of these children were inconsolable. Their screams and cries could be heard everywhere. The soldiers carried out these evil orders with detached brutality because Herod had convinced them that this Child was a threat to *their* security as well.

In his obsession with eliminating the newborn King of the Jews, Herod did not give one thought as to how many tiny, innocent martyrs were to be sacrificed in the process, as long as he got the One that was a possible threat to him.

What he never realized, however, was that the Child he sought so viciously to destroy had already escaped.

My Prayer to God

Lord, I thank You that into the deep engulfing darkness of this world You have come as a light that can never grow dim. All the world has to offer doesn't hold a candle to the light of Your presence. You are a radiant fire that illuminates the shadows of our souls and warms the coldness of our hearts. Just like the Wise Men who followed Your light to find You, I, too, have followed Your light and found You. Now, because I believe in You, Your light dwells within me forever. I have found the way of truth, and my darkness will never be the same. Thank You, Lord, that You can be found by those who seek You. Thank You that those who follow You will never walk in darkness.

In Jesus' name I pray. Amen.

God's Promise to Me

I am the light of the world. He who follows Me
shall not walk in darkness, but have the light of life.

—John 8:12

Chapter Fifteen
The Midnight Flight

Joseph woke suddenly around midnight and took a deep breath. He'd had trouble falling asleep earlier that evening after the Magi left because he kept thinking about what he had overheard them saying to one another. It was something about going home by a different route so they wouldn't have to return to Herod. He wondered what that was all about. When he finally did slip into a deep slumber, he had a vivid yet disturbing dream. From past experience he knew it was a message from God and he should trust it implicitly. Without hesitation he rose to awaken his sleeping wife.

*M*ary, Mary, wake up," he said as he gently shook her shoulder. "An angel of the Lord has just spoken to me in a dream saying we must go to Egypt immediately. Herod is searching for the Child so that he can destroy Him."

Mary rubbed her eyes and sat up.

"I'm sorry, Mary," Joseph continued as he lit one small lamp, "but we must be prepared to stay there until God reveals to us that it's safe to come back."

Hearing the concern in his voice, Mary got up out of bed and went to him.

"Don't worry about leaving Bethlehem, Joseph," she said as she slipped her arms around his waist. "God will be with us wherever we go. We need not fear the future, or where we will stay tonight, or the next night. In God's presence we are always at home."

Joseph hugged her tightly. How he loved this pure and tender woman.

Without further discussion, they dressed and packed everything they could on their faithful donkey, Misha. Mary placed the gold, frankincense, and myrrh on the bottom of the basket with their clothes and bedding on top. In the other basket she packed cooking utensils and as much food as possible. Joseph filled animal skins with water he had drawn from the well earlier that afternoon. When they were ready, he wrote a simple thank-you note to his cousin and placed it on the seat of the chair he had made for him. Then Joseph lifted Mary up onto Misha and handed her the Child, who was snugly wrapped and sound asleep. Mary covered Him with her cloak to protect Him from the chilly night air and keep Him from being seen should anyone happen to observe their sudden departure.

As they made their way quietly through the town, it was a relief to see that every street was completely deserted. Disappearing into the dark covering of the night, they escaped unseen. They traveled all that night and through the next day, straight west until they arrived at the Mediterranean Sea. There they rested. After that they went south to Gaza, then Raphia, and on into Egypt. They felt God guiding their every step and providing for their every need.

Once they arrived in Egypt, they found it to be a safe haven just as it had often been for people during dangerous times. They were able to sell and trade portions of the gifts the Magi had given them, and this provided a tiny home where they could live comfortably. Even though the country was known for its idol worship and godlessness, there was still a sizable Jewish community there, which they found large enough to remain somewhat anonymous within. Joseph's skills as a carpenter were greatly needed and appreciated, so he had ample work. The life they built there was pleasant and quiet and they felt protected. They were determined not to set foot outside of Egypt until God told them it was safe to do so. Several years passed before an angel of the Lord again appeared to Joseph in a dream.

"Get up and take the young Child and His mother to the land of Israel," said the angel. "The men who were trying to kill Him are now all dead."

This time Joseph did not wake Mary in the middle of the night as he had before. He waited until the next morning and told her when she rose to prepare breakfast. They decided they would take the necessary time to ready themselves for this move.

Within a week Joseph had sold his carpentry work and all of the items they could not take with them. He roped Misha to the new cart he had built and loaded it full. With Mary and Jesus, who was now an active young boy, they headed back toward Judea. Joseph reasoned that because Jesus had been born in Bethlehem, perhaps He should be raised there also. Along the way, however, they stopped to buy supplies, and he heard talk that changed his mind.

"Herod died a violent and crazy old man," said the merchant to the customer in front of Joseph as he waited in line to pay. "Some say he deteriorated both physically and mentally with a disease that burned up his insides."

"That's right," the customer agreed as he handed money to the merchant. "I heard he was in total agony his last months because the inside of his body was being eaten away. People said it caused him to smell so bad that no one could stand to come near him. Those who did were not only sickened by his stench but terrorized by his madness as well."

"I say good riddance!" The merchant gave the customer his change. "He finally paid in his body for all the suffering he inflicted on others."

"Excuse me," Joseph said, extending money to the merchant for the small bag of grain he wanted to purchase. "I couldn't help but overhear your conversation. Can you tell me who now reigns in Herod's place?"

"Archelaus is the new king of Judea," responded the merchant. "He is one of the few sons Herod didn't kill. But mark my word, he's every bit as cruel as his father was."

Joseph felt troubled by all he heard. Later that evening, when Jesus was sound asleep, he told Mary his fears about going back to Bethlehem.

"I don't think it's a good idea after all," he said grimly to her.

That night God warned Joseph in a dream that he was not to go back to Judea. When he and Mary got up the next morning, he told her about it.

"I believe we should return to Nazareth," he said. "We have family there. And friends, too. People know us, and it will be easy to settle back into the community."

"You're right, Joseph," Mary agreed. "Jesus can grow up there like a normal child. And have brothers and sisters and play like other boys do. And learn to be a carpenter like you. We can live a safe and quiet life. We will teach Him the Scriptures, and we'll tell Him about His heritage and all the words of prophecy that have been spoken over Him. I want Him to grow strong and be filled with wisdom. The grace of God will be upon Him always, but until the day He is called by His heavenly Father to become the Gift for all mankind He was born to be, I want Him to simply be known as Mary and Joseph's firstborn Son."

My Prayer to God

Lord, I thank You for always guiding me in the way I should go. Thank You that I will never be lost as long as I look to You to lead me. Thank You that no matter where I go, in Your presence I will always be at home. And when I must travel through a dark time, even then night shall be light about me (Psalm 139:11). Just as Mary and Joseph walked according to Your leading and it kept them and what was most valuable to them safe, I pray that I will be as discerning and obedient. I pray that You will keep me on the path of Your perfect will so that I and all I value will be kept safe as well. Enable me to hear You when You tell me to go. Help me to follow wherever You lead. "Let my prayer be set before You as incense, the lifting of my hands as the evening sacrifice" (Psalm 141:2). I worship You and thank You that You came to earth for me.

In Jesus' name I pray. Amen.

God's Promise to Me

Where can I go from Your Spirit? Or where can
I flee from Your presence? If I ascend into heaven,
You are there; If I make my bed in hell, behold,
You are there. If I take the wings of the morning, and
dwell in the uttermost parts of the sea, even there Your
hand shall lead me, and Your right hand shall hold me.

—PSALM 139:7-10

He came to His own, and His own did not receive Him. But as many as received Him, to them He gave the right to become children of God, to those who believe in His name: who were born, not of blood, nor of the will of the flesh, nor of the will of man, but of God.

—JOHN 1:11-13

The Never-Ending Ending

This story, which was heard first in Jerusalem two thousand years ago, has now been carried to all the earth. The Child of the promise, whose birth was foretold centuries before it happened, grew up to be the Messiah the world had long awaited. Elizabeth's son became John the Baptist, an important figure in this great drama, for he would prepare the hearts of the people to receive Jesus as their Savior. And they needed John's help, because Jesus wasn't what they were expecting.

People expected the grand entrance of a king, but Jesus came quietly to a stable. They expected Him to appear to the wealthy and prominent, but He visited the poor and obscure. They looked for fanfare, but that could only be seen in the spirit realm by the humble. He came as what the world needed, but many rejected Him because He wasn't what they wanted.

He became a sanctuary to those who worshiped Him and a snare to those who would not. He was a mirror to reflect the inner workings of the heart, both good and evil. He became hope to those who were hopeless in their pain, sickness, sorrow, and grief. He visited people who had no way out and enabled them to transcend their circumstances. He stood beside the defenseless, to be their champion. He came to people who needed His power, to intervene in their lives and change them forever. Real people like you and me.

God loved us enough to come to earth as a human. To be with us. To prove that He always keeps His promises. To give us eternal life. To have an intimate relationship with us forever. To show us that no matter how dark our world becomes, His Light can never be put out. That's why it's not enough to celebrate His birth only with Christmas lights and decorated trees. We must also celebrate it with His love. For His love lives on forever in those who love Him enough to share it with others. In that way, the story never ends.

Bibliography

The Amplified Bible
Grand Rapids, MI: Zondervan Bible Publishers, 1965.

Blomberg, Craig L. *The New American Commentary—Volumes 22 and 24*.
Nashville, TN: Broadman Press, 1999.

Butler, Trent C. *Holman Bible Dictionary*.
Nashville, TN: Holman Bible Publishers, 1991.

Douglas, J.D. *New Bible Dictionary*.
Wheaton, IL: Tyndale House Publishers, 1985.

Hayford, Pastor Jack W. *Hayford's Bible Handbook*.
Nashville, TN: Thomas Nelson Publishers, 1995.

Hayford, Pastor Jack W. *The Mary Miracle*.
Ventura, CA: Regal Books, 1994.

Hayford, Pastor Jack W. *Spirit-Filled Life Bible, New King James Version*.
Nashville, TN: Thomas Nelson Publishers, 1991.

Henry, Matthew. *Matthew Henry's Commentary on the Whole Bible*.
Peabody, MA: Hendrickson Publishing, Inc. 1991.

Jamieson, Fausset and Brown. *Commentary on the Whole Bible*.
Grand Rapids, MI: Zondervan Publishing House, 1961.

MacDonald, William. *Believer's Bible Commentary*.
Nashville, TN: Thomas Nelson Publishers, 1995.

Peterson, Eugene H. *The Message*.
Colorado Springs, CO: NavPress, 1993.

Smith, Dr. James E. *The Promised Messiah*.
Nashville, TN: Thomas Nelson Publishers, 1993.

Smith, Dr. James E. *What the Bible Teaches About the Promised Messiah*.
Nashville, TN: Thomas Nelson Publishers, 1993.

Tenney, Merrill C. *The Zondervan Pictorial Bible Dictionary*.
Grand Rapids, MI: Zondervan Publishing House, 1967.

A Special
Christmas Gift...
for You!

Make some hot cocoa...light a fire...gather the family...
and spend a few quiet moments together reflecting on
the real reason for the season. Author Stormie Omartian
reads her favorite stories from *The Miracle of Christmas*,
sharing from her heart the true spirit and wonder of this
beautiful time of year.

For your **FREE AUDIO DOWNLOAD** please visit

www.**ChristmaswithStormie**.com

HARVEST
HOUSE